MYTHS ABOUT THE FOUR STAGES OF NIBBANA

Sanghas who misinterpret and go against the lord of the universal Dhamma and the words of the Buddha

By

DR ARIYATHUSHEL ARAHANT

Clever Fox® PUBLISHING

Chennai • Bangalore

CLEVER FOX PUBLISHING
Chennai, India

Published by CLEVER FOX PUBLISHING 2025

ISBN: 978-93-6707-889-1

Homage to the Supremely Enlightened Buddha!

Certainly, Buddha's Dhamma leads to cessation, Nibbana across stages. Buddha is the knower of all worlds, the highest Jewel, the teacher of all perfected ones, homage to the supremely enlightened Buddha!

-Dr Ariyathushel Arahant

The gift of Nirvana Dhamma across stages is an excellent gift, and may you share the right view of higher Dhamma with anyone seeking Buddha's Nirvana freely!

Preface

For a long time, you have been misled and have not understood many things related to the universal Nirvana Dhamma. You have been shown not the noble path, but a path that leads to conventions, continuous suffering and confusion. Though you may believe you are practicing the noble path, it is not truly so. Misguided beliefs stemming from misunderstandings of higher Dhamma, and Sangha matters can obstruct your right view and noble path. There are many myths, and misinterpretations that you are not being told; this book clarifies these matters.

Introduction

When Dhamma is not understood in accordance with the words of the Buddha—meaning the universal four stages of Nirvana Dhamma—you cannot develop the right view or follow the Noble Path.

When Buddha intended one meaning, but the ordinary Sangha interprets it differently, the correct understanding is hindered, leading to wrong views that diverge from the Dhamma. For example, if an ordinary person understands Dhamma merely as a tradition, but the Buddha intended it to refer to the four stages of Nirvana, this difference in interpreting the term Dhamma can lead to a non-noble or incorrect view, which is contrary to the noble path. Similarly, if you understand an ordinary person who gains social ordination as a monk, but Buddha meant a monk as a Sotapanna, Sakadagami, Anagami, and Arahant, the difference in interpreting the word monk itself will lead to a non-noble view or the wrong view in line with the noble path. Keep in mind that Nirvana Dhamma always exists beyond conventional boundaries. This illustrates why the accurate interpretation of the Dhamma is essential for developing the right view. It's not just about the words themselves, but also about the accurate interpretation, each word of Dhamma should be interpreted in accordance with the four stages of Nirvana Dhamma. What is commonly observed is that ordinary Sangha explains Dhamma without any reference to the four stages of Nirvana. Such explanations are at an elementary level of Dhamma and do not help you develop the noble view or right view in accordance with the four stages of Nirvana. This explains why it is only by learning from the noble Sanghas that ordinary Sanghas can cultivate the right view. This is a universal occurrence and an inherent aspect of Dhamma, rather than a socially approved method. Therefore, anyone who calls themselves a follower of the Buddha must learn to understand beyond mere social practices and interpret every word of the Dhamma in relation to the four stages of Nirvana, which transcends conventional understanding. Despite your beliefs or understanding of Dhamma or the Buddha, if you are not aware of or aligned with the universal Dhamma, you are moving away from the teachings of the universal Buddha, Dhamma, and Sangha. To grasp universal Dhamma, you must learn to understand beyond social practices and conventions. If you do not comprehend the basics, such that interpreting universal Dhamma requires understanding beyond mere social practices, you cannot make progress on the noble path. By doing so, you go against the words of the Buddha.

This book discusses issues related to the misinterpretation of Dhamma, and by understanding these misinterpretations, you can eliminate wrong views and develop the right view along the noble path.

Table of Contents

Chapter 1:
Declaration of knowledge

Buddha declared the knowledge of supreme Buddhahood. This declaration helps others know whom to approach when they want to gather specific knowledge; otherwise, they wouldn't know who to ask. Furthermore, the declaration of knowledge of Buddhahood by a person indicates that this individual takes full responsibility for such actions. Not hiding knowledge and not running away from responsibilities are signs of a noble character. Declaring openly and taking personal responsibility for that declaration is truly noble.

Not declaring qualifications—specifically, whether or not one has experienced the four stages of Nirvana—and confidently discussing Dhamma matters while stating things that one does not truly know from personal experience can be misleading to others who are not aware of such in-depth-Dhamma related matters. As a result, both the teachers and the followers remain unaware of higher Dhamma matters. First, there is a need to educate Dhamma teachers. Nirvana Dhamma, as taught by the Buddha, comprises four stages, and that's how you should understand the Buddha's Dharma. The practice involves overcoming the fetters while reflecting the qualities of the universal Triple Gem and honoring the order of "wisdom & merits".

Following in the footsteps of the Buddha, his true Arahant disciples openly declare their knowledge of Arahantship. The only thing you may not have encountered or heard of is a true Arahant as they are extremely rare. When they do appear, you may struggle to recognize them because you have no idea what they look like or what they are truly like. Your mental image of an Arahant does not represent the reality. This explains why many things you have known for centuries are merely representations—such as a look-alike Dhamma, a look-alike Sangha, or a symbol—rather than the real thing or universal Dhamma or universal Sangha.

Chapter 2: Hiding Dhamma matters

You might have heard that some ordinary Sangha members believe that one should not declare Arahantship because it might lead to a shortage of donations received by others. Matters regarding donations could easily be resolved by voluntarily sharing the resources among the community. Hiding higher Dhamma matters for the sake of donations is inappropriate.

Some ordinary Sangha members—those who live in monasteries and homes, running retreats and meditation centers—merely do so to receive donations. They are reluctant to declare that meditation practices do not lead to Nirvana because, for them, securing materials for themselves is a priority. Resources should be shared by everyone.

A person who prioritizes financial matters or donations over Dhamma reflects a mindset that clings to worldly concerns rather than embodying the qualities of a noble disciple of the Buddha. In contrast, one who prioritizes declaring Dhamma matters over personal donations exemplifies the traits of a noble Sangha. Those who fear a lack of material support and donations spread anxiety regarding worldly experiences. This fear stems from greed, hatred, and delusion, which are characteristics of an ordinary state of mind. In contrast, a true Arahant is naturally fearless because they have abandoned greed, hatred, and delusion. Fearlessness is a mental state that arises from relinquishing desires for oneself and others, based on the Dhamma principles of speaking the truth, sharing universal truths, and having confidence in not causing harm to oneself or others. This wisdom enables a genuine Arahant to declare their Arahantship for the well-being of others without pride or expectations of worldly rewards. Sometimes, a person who becomes an Arahant may not even be aware of how they are able to survive, live, or for how long, but such thoughts do not bother them as long as they do their best, considering that life is short for everyone. If you are a genuine practitioner of the Buddha's teachings who wants to support the Buddha and the disciples of the Buddha, you can contribute in any way you can toward the universal Triple Gem, as this will benefit both you and the Sangha community by alleviating suffering. Contribution is a mindset, and appreciating and honoring others doesn't cost anything and doesn't need to be expressed externally. It can be practiced by anyone in their mind, regardless of material status. The noble path to four stages of Nibbana is a training for the mind.

Chapter 3:
Mind state of an Arahant

Words are simply tools to explain Dhamma, food is merely a means to survive, and survival itself is ultimately about sharing higher Dhamma with others, especially for someone who is an Arahant serving Dhamma in the right way, regardless of conventions.

Some people believe that an Arahant can only live in a monastic setting. However, it's important to understand that an Arahant exists in a monastic context regardless, and that monastic context is the final body they embody. What you should understand is that true monasteries are not simply buildings where ordinary people live; they are the physical space of the body, inhabited by individuals who embody the higher Dhamma through their pursuit of enlightenment or four stages of universal Nirvana Dhamma, like the Buddha and the Arahants. This true monastic setting is not defined by physical buildings or spaces where beings bound to samsara reside.

There are two ways to understand a monastic setting. One way is to consider monasteries based on external factors, such as structures made of cement. This is a misguided way of understanding monasteries, and non-noble way. The other way is to understand the mental states that an Arahant experiences, which are not tied to the ten fetters and the final body that supports the residual state. This is the noble way to understand monasteries. This is why you should interpret higher Dhamma and higher Sangha matters in line with the Noble Path.

In general, while some people are eager to visit monasteries, true monasteries serve a deeper purpose by allowing individuals to connect through various modes of communication. Many times, the supreme Buddha visited people to help them experience the four stages of Nirvana Dhamma. The focus should not be on who visits whom, but rather on the importance of individuals gaining a deeper understanding of the higher Dhamma and finding an end to their suffering, which is far more beneficial for spiritual practitioners. This is how you should understand the mental state of an Arahant.

Chapter 4:
Right view

A misguided understanding of Dhamma prevents the attainment of Nibbana. In contrast, having the right view opens the path to Nibbana. Those who seek to understand Nirvana Dhamma should understand the following:

There are no socially accepted frameworks through which you can achieve universal Nirvana. Rather, when your mind becomes free from such things through understanding, you can go beyond limited conventions, and what you already know.

Some individuals attempt to modify surface-level behaviors by following precepts and adhering to cultural expressions like dress codes. However, since Nibbana is an experience beyond social practices and conventions, focusing solely on surface-level behavior and external factors is insufficient for understanding Nibbana. Instead, one should concentrate on understanding the mind states that are not bound by the ten fetters.

A Dhamma sharer or teacher should be capable of explaining the four stages of Nibbana as taught by the Buddha. Understanding these four stages is a universal happening shaped by one's karma and merits is helpful to progress in Nirvana Dhamma. Anyone who explains this Dhamma as expanded by the Buddha represents the teachings of the universal Buddha. Investigating Dhamma knowledge across the four stages of Nibbana—particularly from those who declare Arahantship—provides a reliable way to deepen one's understanding of the noble Sangha and see how they explain higher Dhamma beyond what is commonly known or ordinary Dhamma knowledge in accordance with what the Buddha has taught. This understanding involves utilizing resources for their intended purpose without attachments.

One must learn to use things for their intended purpose without grasping. The purpose of food is to eat; the purpose of clothing is to provide protection for the body; the purpose of medicine is to provide cure for illnesses; the purpose of psychology is to address psychological matters and psychological therapies are for providing therapeutic treatments psychological issues; the purpose of meditation is to provide temporary relief. The use of a lifestyle is to lead a particular life. The purpose of higher Dhamma is to not grasp at the ten fetters and not grasping ten fetters is to not grasp worldly experiences, not grasp worldly experience is to let go of mental pain coming throughs self-view, conventions, social practices, sensual desires desire for formless state and alike. Letting go mental pain from ten fetters is to enhance quality of mind and quality of life and end samsara.

Not understanding the purpose of things that are intended to achieve a goal, or mixing them up, can make it impossible to fulfill that goal. For example, if someone tries to use clothing for food, they cannot satisfy the intended purpose of food, which is to reduce hunger. Conversely, if someone attempts to use food as clothing, they cannot fulfill the intended purpose of clothing, which is to provide protection for the body. Similarly, if someone uses meditation with the aim of achieving Nirvana, they may not reach that goal. This is because the primary purpose of meditation is to provide temporary relief, not to attain Nirvana directly. Those who meditate with the aim of experiencing Nirvana need to expand their practice by reflecting on Dhamma matters and reducing their grasping of self-view and conventions, particularly in daily life while engaging in usual activities.

If a person relies solely on precepts to experience Nirvana, they may only suppress unwholesome behaviors through words and actions without developing the right understanding of themselves, the world, and the universal Triple Gem, which includes the universal Dhamma of Nirvana. While precepts and monastic rules can help an ordinary person maintain wholesome behaviors temporarily through conscious effort, it is essential to extend their practice to develop the right view of the stages of Nirvana Dhamma and the practice itself. Those who appreciate, honor, and support the ordinary Sangha should also expand their practices to include a broader vision that appreciates the universal Sangha, rather than limiting their appreciation to the ordinary Sangha alone. Attaining Nibbana occurs progressively and requires effort. When the right practice is applied, Nibbana can happen unexpectedly.

At times, some members of the Sangha include various subjects in their discussions of Dhamma. Instead of clarifying Nibbana across its stages, they mix Dhamma with personal stories and other topics. As a result, they may develop an understanding of mixed Dhamma, infused with various other subjects, but not a clear understanding of the stages of Nibbana. This is not to say that one should avoid studying other subjects, but rather to emphasize that such topics should not be mixed with universal Dhamma, as each serves different purposes.

Moreover, if someone merely respects and engages with the conventional Sangha, their understanding of the Dhamma is likely to remain at a conventional level, not extending beyond those conventions. Similarly, their merits will only reach a level that an ordinary person can offer to another. By prioritizing conventional Dhamma and the conventional Sangha, one may risk giving less importance to universal Dhamma and universal Sangha. This could lead to growth only within the confines of conventional Dhamma and Sangha, rather than embracing the broader scope of universal Dhamma and universal Sangha. The path to Nibbana and the teachings of the Buddha are realized through the noble Sangha alone. By honoring and appreciating the universal Sangha, you also honor and appreciate the universal Dhamma and the supreme Buddha, the lord of universal Dhamma.

The noble path is a universal practice, not merely related to physical appearances or external factors, nor to individuals as defined by convention. Specifically, a person is subject to change; therefore, instead of grasping at someone as a person, it is more beneficial to utilize the resources they offer, such as higher Dhamma knowledge. This knowledge can help shape right views and cultivate higher merits for the purpose of reducing grasping fetters and developing similar wisdom and qualities within yourself.

Those who don't understand what Buddhahood is often explain the Dhamma by focusing on surface-level and external matters. Some individuals overly emphasize artifacts which are cultural aspects, with a few even making a living from the Dhamma. However, those who genuinely aspire for Nibbana should remember that the purpose of Nibbana is to extinguish desire. This extinguishing of desire occurs when one gives up attachment to the ten fetters. As a result, one's cycle of samsara comes to an end. Thus, the purpose of higher Dhamma is not to profit from it or to gain material wealth or honor; rather, it is essential to let go of all attachments, such as greed, hatred, and delusion, so that the presence or absence of these feelings does not lead to mental suffering caused by likes, dislikes, or expectations surrounding them.

Practicing respect and appreciation for the Triple Gem allows what you appreciate to grow within you, making you embody the Triple Gem. Some ordinary members of the Sangha misinterpret higher Dhamma and matters concerning the higher Sangha, leading to the mistaken view that one should not declare oneself an Arahant, as it may appear to reveal one's ego. This is a misunderstanding. Instead, they should correct their view: declaring oneself an Arahant is appropriate and aligns with higher Dhamma. A genuine Arahant does not feel pride in such declarations. Rather, they offer their insight without clinging to self-view, conventions, precepts, and rituals, and do so without pride, respecting the dignity of others. This approach helps others avoid straying onto the wrong path, enabling them to develop the noble path out of genuine loving-kindness, as a gift.

Noble practice is not based on physical attributes, conventions, or external factors; rather, it is about using the practice for its intended purpose. The identity of the person carrying the higher Dhamma, or the conventional point of view, is not what ultimately matters, as both person and conventions are impermanent. Noble Sangha is not a matter related to flesh meaning you should not cling to these things, but instead use them to progress along the noble path, making use of the noble Sangha to develop higher wisdom and gain merit, ultimately enabling you to extinguish the grasping of self, attachments, and worldly concerns across the stages of Nibbana. Transcending conventions is crucial to understanding the true value of the universal Sangha. When you sharpen your understanding of self, others and the world beyond these conventions, you can experience the universal Nibbana.

Chapter 5:
Differences in mind states

If there were no differences in mind states, there would be little purpose for the Buddha in clarifying and addressing the differences in mental states and how karma and wisdom shapes them. A person born with certain degree of wisdom can learn to grow in wisdom and can learn to shape their karma. There are individual differences in mind states and differences in mind states across four stages of Nirvana. By understanding the distinctions between mental states, one can gain insight into the mind states of Arahants.

Society respects the concept or an idea of an "Arahant", and a true Arahant respects the society and people and all beings. There is no reason to maintain gaps or divisions. Instead, we should use things for their intended purpose. One should associate with noble friends to gain greater wisdom and higher merits without creating divisions or thinking of them as superior, the same, or inferior. In other words, you should be able to utilize things for their intended purpose without grasping. Friendships are maintained on the noble path without grasping to such things or anything. Since you have not encountered those who have completed the noble path, you have not been asked to consider giving up divisions. Instead, you have only been asked to maintain divisions by non-noble Sanghas. To move beyond non-noble ways and reach a noble way of living, one must let go of grasping divisions of any kind. The one who respects people and society reveals the noble qualities.

If applied Dhamma correctly, one should not hurt self or another. Societal practices may not be perfect and can hurt certain categories of people. Suppressing or hurting others is non-Dhamma. Caring for others and their well-being and respecting others is Dhamma. Wealth, access to resources, and dignity-related matters are shared in different ways among people across societies. As a result, some individuals and beings are left to experience various vulnerabilities, whether due to poverty, disability, social background, health issues including mental health issues, various life's circumstances, and like wise. Therefore, practicing the noble path requires one to think and act beyond conventional ways.

When speaking the truth, it's sometimes evident among some of the ordinary Sangha members, including those living in monastic settings, that they may travel around the world spending money on tours for social gatherings and events. However, some donors within spiritual communities may struggle to afford their next meal. Instead, those who aspire to practice the noble path should, if they have sufficient funds, try and distribute whatever they can afford to distribute among the community and people of any background and beings after ensuring they have enough for their basic needs, a noble practice.

You may hear these words of Dhamma, and to apply within you, it requires you to make yourself strong enough to uphold the Dhamma in places where it is lacking and to go beyond the common ways of thinking and doing while renouncing common practices. A common belief among spiritual practitioners is the respect for the concept or an idea of an Arahant. Since it is rare to hear about or meet Arahants in everyday life, many may not fully understand the mind state of Arahants. However, Arahants, who have transcended conventional ways, show immense respect and care for all people, regardless of their backgrounds or beliefs.

The common way may lead to sadness when losing things, while the noble way teaches us not to become sad about losses, as, in the end, we all lose everything in life anyway at death. Embracing this truth, one awakens to true life experiences and develops wisdom and noble qualities, which help reduce clinging to self-view and conventions, and social practices while honoring the universal Triple Gem and maintain the noble precepts is the practice one must adopt to become a Sotapanna.

Chapter 6:
Social support and universal support

Typically, Arahants who have given up desire for worldly experiences do not just prioritize the Dhamma; they also do not concern themselves with what happens in the future. When they need to do something in the present, they do it without attachment or anxiety about the outcome. They often act without knowing how they will finish a task. If an Arahant has any resources, they use those resources to share the Dhamma, even if they know they may not have material support to eat the next meal tomorrow. Nonetheless, they accept life as it evolves, prioritizing the Dhamma because it benefits those who are suffering. This is how an Arahant functions.

There is a myth perpetuated by some ordinary members of the Sangha that they must avoid misinterpreting the Buddha's universal Dhamma, as such misunderstandings could lead to their downfall in samsara and hinder the development of right view. One such myth arose from the comment made by ordinary monk Nagasena, suggesting that Arahants can only survive in monastic settings. This implies that when one becomes an Arahant, if they do not live in a monastic setting, which is typically constructed from materials like cement and other physical substances, they cannot survive for more than seven days. However, this practice raises questions about its alignment with the Buddha's teachings. Instead, what you should understand is that monasticism is not merely an external environment; it pertains to the inner state or the final body borne by an Arahant on the noble path. This explains why the Buddha recommended that when individuals of noble lineage or those who have attained Buddhahood—such as Tathagata, Paccekabuddha, and Arahant—pass away, monuments should be erected in their honor. These monuments serve as a way for others to accumulate merit by paying respects to these figures, thereby creating a meaningful place of worship.

Some ordinary Sangha over centuries have attempted to create a distorted image of the perfected Buddha by misinterpreting the Dhamma. For example, when someone claims that the Buddha recommended women in monastic settings to respect all men simply because they have the form of a man, this is a form of sexism or a discrimination towards woman. However, sexism is often related to form, and those who are enlightened through the four stages of Nirvana do not grasp form, as attachment to form has been abandoned during the training on the path to Arahantship. Buddhas do not say one should respect another merely because of external factors, but because of their right view. Whoever has the right view should be honored and respected regardless of their form; this is how you should understand the Buddha's teachings.

There should be no doubts: there is no one in this world who wishes to treat and protect women as much as the Supreme Buddha does. This understanding reflects the perfect wisdom and infinite kindness of the universal Buddha. Both women and men, as well as all beings, deserve to be treated with respect and protection. This is a fundamental lesson that the Supreme Buddha taught us, his universal disciples. You can also learn to cultivate these noble qualities within yourself. This can be discussed as below:

If someone claims that men are better, the same as, or worse than women or vice versa, they are only suggesting part of their nature is superior, similar, or inferior to the other part. This is because all men and woman are created by a mother and a father, and men and women are integral to everyone's nature. While certain characteristics of a particular form may be better suited for specific roles, this suitability does not mean that one gender is superior, same or inferior to another. Even the strongest men and women do not remain the same; they are also subject to change. Instead, one should appreciate, respect and care all beings. Welcoming whatever contributions men or women can offer to society in various ways is a way of training in the universal noble path. For example, by being a good parent, one man and woman may be able to gift a child to society through parenthood, while another man may offer basics of the teachings of the Buddha as a conventional monk, another man may offer cleaning services as a cleaner, and another woman may provide legal services as a lawyer or share their musical talents. Whenever anyone contributes in their own way to the well-being of themselves and others, they are practicing the Dhamma trough their efforts in contributing to the society. This explains why there are no unusual things to do in the noble path but to apply wisdom, and noble qualities within your daily roles, and daily activities. Conventional Sangha may explain the basic Dhamma and introduce you to preliminary Dhamma practices. In contrast, the noble Sangha will explain the higher Dhamma, including the four stages of universal Nirvana. However, this is not meant to suggest that one is superior, inferior, or the same as the other; rather, in the path leading to cessation or Nirvana, it is about utilizing

Dhamma and Sangha for their intended purpose without grasping or hurting anyone.

Karma cannot be generalized. An Arahant can die regardless of whether they are in a monastic or non-monastic setting as seen from a conventional perspective when it is their time to go. Nibbana goes beyond conventions. In the end, everyone dies. Just as a deadly air crash can have survivors, some individuals with advanced cancer may continue to live. Therefore, it is incorrect and a misinterpretation of the Dhamma to assert that Arahants will inevitably die within seven days after attaining Arahantship if they do not live in monasteries made of cement and other materials. What you should understand is that the kindest and wisest of all, the universal Buddha, would never make a disciple suffer or die merely because they completed their training. Those who claim that an Arahant dies within seven days after achieving enlightenment are attempting to create a negative image of the universal Buddha. You must not associate with those who try to tarnish the reputation or depict imperfect qualities of the supreme Buddha. Instead, strive to recognize and appreciate the perfect qualities of the universal Buddha.

Apart from observing your thoughts and learning to let go of self-view and misconceptions, it is essential to develop a correct understanding of the perfect Buddha, perfect Dhamma, and perfect Sangha to experience stream entry (Sotapanna). Understanding the perfect qualities of the universal Triple Gem will help you release your attachments, which is what we mean by taking refuge in the universal Triple Gem on the noble path. This does not simply mean uttering the phrases "I take refuge in the Triple Gem" without a true understanding of what the Triple Gem represents. The more you get to know the Triple Gem, the closer you will come to universal Nirvana Dhamma.

Death is primarily influenced by individual karmic factors. Generalizations must be avoided, and one should not misinterpret the Buddha's Dhamma. Even literature does not support such myths. For example, an old man and a woman achieved Arahantship and passed away not within seven days, but after several weeks due to natural aging—an event unrelated to their experience of Arahantship (see Dhp 225).

You must avoid taking incorrect views expressed by misguided disciples or those who are not true disciples, instead you mays hear Dhamma from true disciples such as

Sotapanna, Sakadagami, Anagami, and Arahant. This is essential because the higher Nirvana Dhamma is sublime, difficult to understand, rare to hear, and cannot be confined to social practices, rituals, and conventions. It can only be fully comprehended by those who experience it through the four stages of Nirvana. Those who genuinely appreciate and honor the Buddha can learn to interpret the Dhamma, which the Buddha worked diligently to present to us. It is the best means of alleviating mental distress caused by life's difficulties. To experience Nirvana through Dhamma in life, one must understand that life's difficulties are a part of experiencing existence. It is only after you have encountered enough life experiences, especially the painful ones, that you develop an understanding being mentally affected does not necessarily change circumstances, you can develop the ability to remain unaffected by them. Instead, you should focus on addressing things wisely. If you can understand the basics of the noble path, you will be able to develop it further.

To come to such an understanding, you must realize that clinging to life experiences is meaningless, and the pain can be difficult to bear. Thus, to practice, you must apply the Dhamma by "thinking and doing" beyond conventional ways within your daily life. We are not following the conventional path to becoming a monk, but rather the universal route to achieving a state of mind that does not grasp at fetters; universal monk route. The universal monk route holds no value to external factors but to mind states. Among all the paths available for becoming a monk, this universal training emphasizes a key aspect: a monk is someone who does not cling to their life experiences or become attached to the sensory information of the world around them. Instead, they focus on transcending external factors and their impact on their lives. This teaching was imparted to all of the Buddha's followers not just for followers of a specific tradition, country, lifestyle and alike. If you claim to be a follower of the Buddha and genuinely respect Buddha's teachings, the best thing you can do is learn what the universal Buddha has taught to both humans and gods: the training path that leads to the four stages of universal Nirvana Dhamma.

If any interpretation of the Dhamma leads to the death of a genuine person who has completed their training, it should be understood as a version of the Dhamma fabricated by ordinary people or ordinary Sangha, rather than what the Buddha actually taught or the true Dhamma. If any experience of the Dhamma leads to a temporary escape from mental distress, such as through meditation practices developed after the Buddha's Parinirvana—including modern day samatha, vipassana, jhana practices, and similar methods—it should be understood as a version of the Dhamma fabricated by ordinary people or a conventional Sangha, rather than what the Buddha actually taught or the true Dhamma. Similarly, if any interpretation of the Sangha is bascd on external appearances, the environment, and social conventions, it should be considered a version created by ordinary people or a conventional Sangha, rather than the authentic Sangha established by the Buddha or the true Sangha on the noble path. Those who genuinely appreciate and honor the Buddha may learn to interpret the universal Dhamma, which the Buddha devoted much effort to presenting to us. First, it is crucial to recognize that ultimately, everyone dies, but the circumstances surrounding death can vary among individuals. Achieving Arahantship does not change the inevitability of death. Second, the Dhamma of Nirvana across four stages enables us to let go of mental distress in a stable manner. This is not merely a meditation practice, but rather an in-depth approach that includes several components and needs to be practiced consistently within daily life. Furthermore, the term 'Sangha' in the noble path refers to states of mind that are not grasping at external factors. You may learn these three points to clarify and distinguish between fabricated Dhamma and true Dhamma, as well as between a conventional Sangha and the true Sangha. The matters related to the true Sangha are discussed not to undermine the ordinary Sangha but to show them how they can develop beyond what they currently know in order to become part of the noble Sangha.

As pointed out, what you should know is that there are twisted stories, lies, and misinterpretations that obscure the true teachings, revealing the hidden gem of universal Nirvana Dhamma. If any interpretation of the Dhamma contradicts this understanding, it should be recognized as a human concoction, a version of Dhamma and Sangha created by ordinary Sangha during some point of time in the history or now but such things are not the authentic teachings of the Buddha. This is how you should understand the supreme Dhamma, which embodies the best of everything taught to us by the supreme Buddha. If you can understand Dhamma and Sangha as interpreted by the Buddha, that is how you can develop in the Buddha' noble path.

Chapter 7:
Rituals

Sometimes people can get trapped in rituals, merely following them as seen from the outside without necessarily committing to reducing their self-view within, or they may hold the wrong view. That can make it difficult for them to purify from self. This demonstrates that spiritual practice cannot be generalized solely based on external factors such as the rituals people follow, their traditions, settings, dress codes, or social practices. Each person's spiritual journey is deeply personal, rooted in the sincere commitment to let go of attachments in their minds, often referred to as fetters, as they progress through the stages of Nibbana. Universal Nibbana encourages a practice of self-purification that is not reliant on external factors but focuses on cleansing one's inner thoughts. By understanding how the universe operates—bringing both ups and downs to each individual, along with the impermanence of self, others, and the world—one can recognize the futility of clinging to worldly experiences. This clinging often leads to mental suffering and is not worth the pain it causes. By awakening to true life experience, applying wisdom, a person may reflect on the Dhamma repeatedly until they progress through the four stages of Nibbana.

An individual experiences self and the world personally within the self. One cannot experience self out of self in others or in the world. Every individual is born with unique characteristics and is exposed to unique experiences. Only by taking self-responsibility for one's intentional actions, constantly practicing reducing grasping self-view and social practices while reflecting the universal Triple Gem as a friend is there a route to escape and become free from karma, stress, and mental pain coming from self. That is why rules taken as a ritualistic practice are not enough because people can engage in doing external things without necessarily applying Dhamma in their thoughts, words, and actions. One who wants to practice universal Dhamma should purify thoughts, words and actions from pride, excessive dislikes, and excessive likes towards life experiences.

Practitioners of Dhamma should develop wisdom to let go of things that are gone, avoid excessively worrying in worrisome situations but apply wisdom to resolve things that can be resolved, fulfil responsibilities, avoid acting or pretending for various reasons, including to gain others' approval and the like, avoid defining self-identity by letting go of the need to compare one another, avoid degrading others to make self-feel better about self, and avoid unfair treatment of others and the like while appreciating, reflecting, and attending to the universal Triple Gem who have perfected in Dhamma to various leaves across the four stages of Nibbana and the disciples who have perfected in wisdom as revealed to them by the universal Buddha, including the trainees.

Chapter 8:
Outsider path and the outsider disciples

The path to Nibbana contains two ways, which bridge an ordinary person to a noble person. There is an outsider path or the outsider disciples who are training to become insider disciples or the noble path, and there is an insider path of trainees (Sotapanna, Sakadagami, Anagami) and perfected ones or Arahants.

Typically, outsider disciples can grasp identifying themselves in line with social standards, one as superior to another and the like. The outsider path is not perfect and is full of conventions. Thus, among those outsiders, those who are wise enough to comprehend the possible role that karma plays in Nibbana and are willing to test whether the possibility is true or false can progress into entering Nibbana if they strengthen their practice in the right manner.

Outsider disciples need to understand how to link an outsider's training path to an insider path. By dropping imperfections and letting go of grasping the fetters while reflecting the universal Triple Gem, a person from any conventional background can reduce grasping fetters. This explains why Dhamma is to be taken as a raft. In the end, all conventions become the same across the four stages of Nibbana. Thus, dropping conceit, not comparing by saying I am better, worse or the same and not dividing others and similar practices strengthen people to stop in self-inflicting pain and to walk through the universal noble path to experience blissful Sotapanna.

"And what, bhikkhus, is right view? Right view, I say, is twofold: there is right view that is affected by taints, partaking of merit, ripening in the acquisitions; and there is right view that is noble, taintless, supramundane, a factor of the path.

"And what, bhikkhus, is right view of an ordinary person, outsider disciple that is affected by the taints, partaking of merit, ripening in the acquisitions? 'There is what is given and what is offered and what is sacrificed; there is fruit and result of good and bad actions; there is this world and the other world; there is mother and father; there are beings who are reborn spontaneously; there are in the world good and virtuous spiritual practitioners and leaders who have realised for themselves by direct knowledge and declare this world and the other world.' This is right view affected by taints, partaking of merit, ripening in the acquisitions.

"And what, bhikkhus, is right view that is noble, taintless, supramundane, a factor of the path known by noble ones? The wisdom, the faculty of wisdom, the power of wisdom, the investigation-of-states enlightenment factor, the path factor of right view in one whose mind is noble, whose mind is taintless, who possesses the noble path and is developing the noble path: this is right view that is noble, taintless, supramundane, a factor of the path.

"One makes an effort to abandon wrong view and to enter upon right view: this is one's right effort. Mindfully one abandons wrong view, mindfully one enters upon and abides in right view: this is one's right mindfulness. Thus, these three states run and circle around right view, that is, right view, right effort, and right mindfulness."

- Mahācattārīsakasutta, MN 117

The insider path is perfect with no grasping conventions, and insiders understand the four stages of Nibbana progressively through experience. Thus, Arahant merely declare attainment without grasping self-view and standard social practices so that they provide respect to others without asking anything including respect for themselves.

The decline of Dhamma over the centuries has seen people are understanding only the outsider path and not the insider path. During Buddha' time, people were educated about the four stages of Nibbana, but in modern days, people are least educated about the four stages of Nibbana.

"...When beings are deteriorating in Dhamma practice and the true Dhamma and true Sangha are disappearing there are more conventional Sangha but few noble sangha coming from various backgrounds. Kassapa, the true Dhamma does not disappear so long as a counterfeit of the true Dhamma has not arisen in the world. But when a counterfeit of the true Dhamma arises in the world, then the true Dhamma disappears..."

- Saddhammappatirūpakasutta, SN 16.13

Chapter 9: Answering with no qualifications

When asked Dhamma related questions, many people answer questions without qualification in that they do not understand Sotapanna to Arahant through experience in daily life. Given individual differences in karma, one thing a person who wants to understand universally applicable Dhamma should do is not to generalise and say that those who live in a particular setting (i.e., monastic), country, gender, and the like can experience Nibbana better than others. Such statements contradict Dhamma. Some people make statements that are wrong, such as that Nibbana can be exclusively experienced by a particular group of people, because they don't think karma has a role to play in Nibbana. Although an ordinary person may not comprehend karma and rebirth fully, they can hear the confirmation of such things as true from those Arahants who have developed triple knowledge.

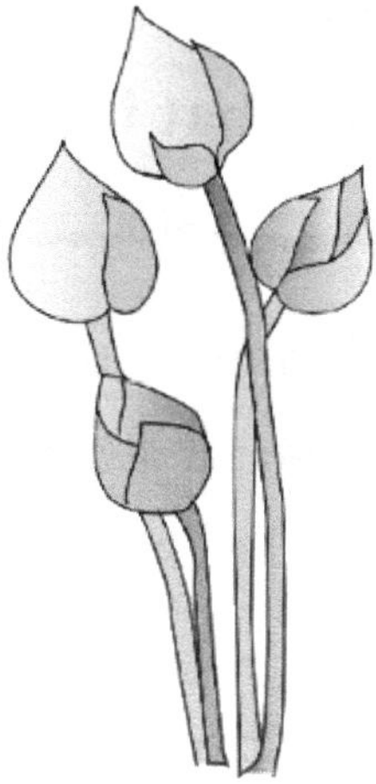

Chapter 10:
What if?

You may adopt a mode of discovery and seek answers to valuable questions; what if a spiritual path suggests that there is no such a thing called universal ways of functioning and karma, a sensible person would think that there is no point in following a spiritual practice, giving to noble people, treating parents and not dividing people, etc. This is because, if a certain practice suggests that there is no karma, by following such a spiritual practice and not following a spiritual practice, a person can attain exactly the same (gain or not gain things in the same manner).

If a spiritual path suggests that there is no root cause that make people impurified and suffer, people suffer without a reason. A sensible person may think that, if there is no root cause of purification from sufferings, those who are purified and not purified are faced with the same outcome/destiny, and there is reason to follow such a spiritual practice.

If a spiritual path suggests that karma does not increase or decrease due to what you do, there is a fixed soul and, in that case, a person who should reject following such a path on the ground that those who follow a spiritual path and those who do not follow attain the same.

Take a spiritual life that merely relies on logic and enquiry, but, among what they teach others, a sensible person can find some things are logical, and some things are not logical. Thus, such a spiritual life is unreliable, and a sensible person should leave an unreliable path.

Take a spiritual practice that claims to bring perfection, but you hear imperfect practices. Such a spiritual practice is unreliable and not genuine, and it can't be Buddha's perfect practice. A sensible person should leave such practices.

If a member of the Sangha suggests that Nibbana is merely a convention and that it depends on external conventions, then when those conventions change, Nibbana should also change. Similarly, if a member of the Sangha argues that Nibbana depends on the external environment, then when that environment changes, a person's state of Nibbana should also shift. In this case, Nibbana would not be a stable experience as understood by the Buddha. A sensible person should avoid drawing conclusions from such a perspective, as traditions, rituals, and lifestyles evolve.

Conversely, if a member of the Sangha asserts that Nibbana lies beyond conventions and can be experienced in the mind independently of these conventions or external factors, then Nibbana, which does not rely on changing conventions, is likely to be stable. The Buddha has taught us a stable method for escaping suffering, rather than just a temporary relief. A sensible person should seek guidance from those who understand this stable path.

Chapter 11: Intentional dividing

Intentionally dividing universal Dhamma and universal Sangha is one of the six major offences a person can commit during their lifetime that will prevent Nibbana. Those who are genuinely seeking Nibbana should understand that those who divide Buddha's universal Dhamma and those who make Dhamma appear to be limited Dhamma or imperfected Dhamma are not the disciples of Buddha.

"It is impossible, it cannot happen, for a stream entrant to divide the (universal Dhamma or) community of Sangha"

-AN 1.268

Yet, you have commonly heard that some of those who commit major offences by dividing Dhamma and Sangha tell you not to commit minor offences and receive offerings from you. It is not nature that leads to the disappearance of Nibbana or the four stages of Dhamma but ignorant acts of dividing universal Dhamma among unwise people or Sangha communities who don't care, appreciate or value universal Buddha, universal Dhamma and universal Sangha.

"There are five things, Kassapa, that lead to the longevity of the true Dhamma; Nibbana, to its nondecay and nondisappearance. What are the five? Here the ordinary people (monks and householders) dwell with reverence and deference towards the universal Buddha; they dwell with reverence and deference towards the universal Dhamma (Nibbana); they dwell with reverence and deference towards the universal Saṅgha; they dwell with reverence and deference towards the universal noble training; they dwell with reverence and deference towards universal noble concentration. These, Kassapa, are the five things that lead to the longevity of the true Dhamma, to its nondecay and nondisappearance."

- Saddhammappatirūpakasutta, SN 16.13

Drinking alcohol and engaging in activities to break five precepts are minor offences. This explains why even people like Aṅgulimāla (Angulimala Sutta, MN 86) and drunkards like Sarakaani (Sarakaani Sutta, SN 55.24) could experience Nibbana but some of the ordinary monk such as Devadatta (Dhp 163) could not experience Nibbana. That is not to say continue engaging in breaking precepts but not to worry too much if you happened to break them in the past. You may correct them now and engage in wholesome deeds, as it will still allow you to experience cessation from pain that self brings to you, which is the blissful Nibbana.

The four stages of Nibbana are the teachings of Buddha that are carried out by senior Sangha meaning Arahants. A person who used to divide universal Dhamma and universal Sanga may rectify their mistake not to do that again. By ignoring past mistakes and admitting one's mistakes in the presence of Buddha or senior Sangha of Arahants, apologizing for one's mistakes, ignoring minor matters but focusing only on major offences, the community of Sangha can flourish in their practice in preparation to experiencing four-fold Nibbana. This is the interpretation of Sāmagāmasutta, MN 104;

"Then Sotapanna Ānanda and Cunda went to the Buddha, bowed, sat down to one side, and Ānanda informed him of what Cunda had said. He went on to say, "Sir, it occurs to me: 'When the Buddha has passed away, let no dispute arise in the Saṅgha. For such a dispute would be for the detriment and suffering of the people, against the people, for the harm, detriment, and suffering of gods and humans."

"What do you think, Ānanda? Do you see even two individual's whose understanding differs among the noble sangha communities regarding the things I have taught from my direct knowledge, that is, the four kinds of reflection a Sotapanna can practice to gain Anagami state, the four right efforts, the four bases of psychic power, the five faculties, the five powers, the seven awakening factors, and the noble eightfold path?"

"No, sir, I do not. Nevertheless, there are some ordinary people who has no direct knowledge of Dhamma, and they appear to live obedient to the Buddha, but when the Buddha has passed away they might create a dispute in the Saṅgha regarding monastic life style or livelihood or the monastic practice. Such a dispute would be for the detriment and suffering of the people, against the people, for the harm, detriment, and suffering of gods and humans."

"Ānanda, dispute about monastic lifestyle or livelihood or the monastic code is a minor matter. But should a dispute arise in the Saṅgha concerning the universal noble path or the noble practice leading to four stages of Nibbana, that would be for the detriment and suffering of the people, against the people, for the harm, detriment, and suffering of gods and humans.

Ānanda, there are these six roots of arguments within the community of Sangha. What six? Firstly, a person is irritable and acrimonious. Such a person lacks respect and reverence for the universal Buddha, universal Dhamma and universal Saṅgha, and they don't fulfill the four stages of training (i.e. Sotapanna etc.). They create a dispute in the community of Saṅgha, which is for the detriment and suffering of the people, against the people, for the harm, detriment, and suffering of gods and humans. If you see such a root of arguments in yourselves or others, you should try to give up this bad thing. If you don't see it, you should practice so that it doesn't come up in the future. That's how to give up this bad root of arguments, so it doesn't come up in the future.

Furthermore, a person is offensive and contemptuous ... They're jealous and stingy ... They're devious and deceitful ... They have corrupt wishes and wrong view ... They're attached to their own views, holding them tight, and refusing to let go. Such a person lacks respect and reverence for the universal Buddha, universal Dhamma and universal Saṅgha, and they don't fulfill the four stages of training. They create a dispute in the community of Saṅgha, which is for the detriment and suffering of the people, against the people, for the harm, detriment, and suffering of gods and humans. If you see such a root of arguments in yourselves or others, you should try to give up this bad thing. If you don't see it, you should practice so that it doesn't come up in the future. That's how to give up this bad root of arguments, so it doesn't come up in the future."

- Sāmagāmasutta, MN 104

Most people don't know the precise information about the four stages of Nibbana. Someone who has directly experienced the four stages of Nibbana can tell you the precise information, and they are the Arahant disciples of the Buddha, especially if they don't grasp fetters such as social practices, etc.

What have some of the Sangha been committing over the centuries? Major offenses, if they divide Dhamma or Sangha intentionally. Likely, there are genuine people among Sangha, who divide Dhamma or Sangha without knowing it is a major offense, and, likely, they may not intend to divide Dhamma. This is their call. Such practitioners should stop intentionally dividing Dhamma and Sangha for their wellbeing and for the wellbeing of others in the universal Buddha's path.

Practicing Dhamma should mean you learn to give priority to the universal Triple Gem. When people do not honor and respect universal Triple Gem including the "wisdom & merit" order as they should, they abandon wisdom and merits that they need gathering to progress in the noble path. In doing so, they are unable to experience four stages of universal Nirvana Dhamma.

Mind states among some ordinary Sangha can be offensive, arrogant or condescending. Some can be jealous and stingy. Some can be devious and deceitful. Some can have corrupt wishes and wrong views. Some can be attached to their own view so that, when they hear something new, they might struggle to update their knowledge. People who possess these qualities within monastic or nonmonastic communities, regardless of where they live, can divide universal Dhamma and have no appreciation or respect for universal Buddha, universal Dhamma or universal Sangha. If you see yourself contributing to dividing Dhamma or Sangha, you should try amending what you do and try not to divide Dhamma or Sangha hereafter. That will be of lasting welfare for you.

"One way to recognize an Arahant is to say that they know Buddha is the knower of all through personal experience: "This, brahmin, is what is called 'a footprint of the Realized One' and also 'a trace of the Realized One' and also 'a mark of the Realized One'. At this point a noble disciple has not yet come to a conclusion, but they are coming to the conclusion., 'The Blessed One is a fully awakened Buddha...."

-Cūḷahatthipadopamasutta, MN 27

Chapter 12: Freedom from monastic rules and precepts

For a long time, you have understood monastic rules and precepts, and the principles of "sila, samadhi, and panna" are considered a threefold training that leads to enlightenment across the four stages of Nirvana Dhamma. If you are to learn something new now, it should be something beyond what you already know.

What lies beyond monastic rules and precepts are noble virtues. Noble virtues can only be developed by letting go of grasping self-view and social practices based on the illusion that things are stable. In addition, one should take refuge in the Triple Gem as much as possible. Thus, when someone says that developing sila, samadhi, and panna is the way to experience the noble path, it is not meant to indicate monastic rules or precepts, concentrated meditations such as jhanas, or the wisdom that an ordinary person possesses. Rather, it refers to the sila or virtue associated with a Sotapanna or Sakadagami. The noble virtues of a Sotapanna or Sakadagami are what is meant by developing sila on the noble path.

Typically, when someone undertakes a spiritual practice (including precepts and similar commitments), it involves both pleasure and pain. This is because maintaining the practice requires effort, which inherently involves some degree of discomfort. This applies to an ordinary person. The ordinary mind, functioning in line with habitual thinking, becomes attached to worldly experiences—experiencing both the highs and lows of life that bring about feelings of pleasure and pain.

After one gains Sotapanna, the pain that comes when attempting to follow a spiritual practice disappears, because the right view gained at the Sotapanna state makes a person naturally possess noble virtues, which means that no effort or pain is needed to maintain precepts or to apply wisdom to maintain a balanced mind state while retaining sensual pleasures. Thus, the middle way is a comfortable abiding. This explains why there is no need to do unusual things, like walking without shoes, meditating in a certain posture day and night; all that is required is applying the right practice in the right strength to progress to the right view. The right view meaning the view of the noble ones that can be developed by hearing the true Dhamma from Arahants and reflecting day and night while doing other things. In this way, the training path becomes a natural and comfortable abiding.

Chapter 13:
Understanding sensory pleasures

Some degree of enjoyment comes from sensory experiences. Thus, people keep liking them more and more. Liking them, since birth, everyone tends to enjoy such things.

Yet, life experiences teach a lesson that all get to experience what they like as well as dislike. Understanding that what you like and dislike can happen, a person can develop wisdom to reduce too much liking the worldly experiences. That understanding allows you to enjoy experiences without liking and disliking or expecting things out of your experiences. This makes it possible for you to enjoy worldly experiences with stability, a better enjoyment than ordinary ways of enjoying.

Unstable enjoyment is a common experience, while stable enjoyment is considered a noble pursuit. To transition from ordinary enjoyment to noble enjoyment, try to reflect on the Dhamma in your daily life. By contemplating and applying the Dhamma in your everyday activities, you will facilitate your experience of Nirvana within your life. If you treat the Dhamma as a separate matter, such as setting aside time during your routine activities solely for meditation and reflection on Dhamma, that may not be sufficient and might not have the desired impact on your experience. Instead, you should extend your Dhamma practice to incorporate a deeper understanding of life experiences in your daily activities. Similarly, if you find yourself overly carried away or disturbed by external factors to the point where you cannot reduce your desires when encountering beautiful things, simply closing your eyes is not a strong enough approach to training. You cannot always keep your eyes shut, if you have to run away from beautiful things and this limited practice will not effectively diminish your desires. Instead, aim to keep your eyes open but cultivate the ability to remain unaffected by both beautiful and ugly occurrences around you. This way, sensory information won't trouble you, even when you are keeping your sensory information coming. To develop higher Dhamma, there is no need to retreat as separate activity or go to the forest or set aside your regular activities to apply the Dhamma; rather, you should develop the ability to reduce grasping and attachments to worldly experiences coming from sensory information in your everyday life through your usual activities.

Relying solely on retreats or meditation practices for developing a higher understanding of Dhamma is limiting and insufficient for truly experiencing the teachings in daily life. This explains why even among ordinary Sangha members who live in monasteries and spend years in meditation or attending various retreats, they may not experience universal Nirvana Dhamma. It is the practices that lead to universal Nirvana Dhamma, and those who live in monasteries and homes can experience the fourfold Nirvana Dhamma, but not simply because they reside in a monastery or a home.

To progress along the noble path, it is important to understand that by supporting and assisting the noble Sangha in their Dhamma activities, you can cultivate the innate wisdom and merits within you, in accordance with the universal laws of Dhamma and karma. This is the only way to develop the higher wisdom and merits necessary to experience the universal Nirvana Dhamma for ordinary practitioners of the Sangha.

Anyone who experiences Arahantship will declare their attainment out of compassion, genuine care, and loving kindness towards their spiritual friends. If someone interprets the declaration of Arahantship from a true Arahant as a matter of ego, they misunderstand the nobility of Dhamma and the Sangha. Conversely, those who recognize that a person can make such declarations without pride or ego—just as the Buddha and Arahants have done throughout the centuries—possess a correct understanding of the mind state of Arahants, as well as the higher Dhamma and Sangha matters.

There are two approaches to consider. One way is to support and honor the individuals who live in monasteries. The other way involves supporting the Buddha's Dhamma, which means identifying errors and guiding individuals along the noble path so that they can improve themselves. This approach also includes prohibiting or removing those in monasteries who do not adhere to the right view, who are not disciplined in line with Dhamma Vinaya (i.e. Sotapanna etc.), and who do not follow the noble path toward purifying the Dhamma and the Sangha. This effort, which involves higher Dhamma principles, is discussed to assist those who live in monasteries and homes in achieving universal Nirvana Dhamma. It is not intended as a form of dislike or hatred toward them as individuals. Instead, it explains subject matters with the intent to open the universal noble path based on right view; this is how you should understand the mind state of Arahants. It's important to learn how to gather wisdom and merit along the way. Practicing Dhamma should mean you learn to give priority to the universal Triple Gem.

Chapter 14:
Life experience

Each individual should understand that grasping life experiences produces pain based on their life experiences, which they are willing to like and dislike. In the path to Nirvana Dhamma, many aspects of life experience need to be understood. This explains why people who are literate can attain Nirvana Dhamma. Nowadays, there are many scholars, yet even as a scholar, you might struggle to understand Dhamma through life experience alone. No amount of scholarly knowledge can help you reduce the mental distress that arises from life. That is not to say that becoming a scholar is not worthwhile; you may pursue scholarship if you wish. However, it is crucial to prioritize alleviating pain and suffering in samsara, regardless of one's scholarly status, as the training path that leads to fourfold Nirvana remains the same for all.

When you experience pleasures, take a moment to reflect on their impermanence, realizing that they cannot last forever. As a result, your expectations for worldly pleasures may diminish over time depending on the strength of your practice. Thus, when these pleasures wane, your understanding will help prevent excessive worries or distress.

Stable enjoyment is a noble path. A Sotapanna experiences a blessed day and night through experiences without attachment and delightful sensual pleasures. Nibbana is an understanding based on wisdom. There's no point in not enjoying sensual pleasures, as life is short. It would be wise to experience the best; therefore, you may eat well, sleep well, dress nicely, and take good care of yourself and others as much as possible while applying Dhamma in daily life.

Remember that universal Nirvana Dhamma is a step by step process, and universal Nirvana Dhamma does not necessitate an ascetic lifestyle where one consumes little or nothing, as these practices do not lead to Nirvana Dhamma. This explains why the Buddha abandoned strict ascetic practices before attaining the middle way, which involves no extreme austerity. Even in monasteries or similar places where individuals strive to commit training to experience Nirvana Dhamma, having access to good food and adequate self-care will support their training path. Why? Because when you are provided with sufficient comforts, if you are satisfied with such things, you are less likely to seek excessive physical pleasures such as food and material goods, allowing your mind to move beyond attachment to these things.

When a mind is not satisfied with certain things, you tend to seek more. However, when you become satisfied and have enough, you stop seeking such things by human nature. In this way, those who have had sufficient materials, honor, and worldly experiences may find it easier to not seek such things anymore across stages of Nirvana Dhamma. However, one thing to remember is that "sufficient comfort" is a subjective process. Each individual should feel satisfied with the comforts they have and be content regardless of what may be seen as sufficient or insufficient by a third party.

If you understand Nirvana Dhamma as a socially constructed aspect of life or a concept, that is a limited understanding. This is because Nirvana Dhamma is not merely a socially constructed concept; religion, tradition, or a socially constructed aspect such as a monastic lifestyle, or any external lifestyle. Rather, Nibbana is a universal phenomenon where some beings are born into a state of Nirvana Dhamma at their mental continuum. This is how you should comprehend the universal Dhamma as taught by the universal Buddha.

"It's possible that wanderers of other religions might say: 'The ascetic Gotama spoke of the cessation of perception and feeling, and he includes it in happiness. What's up with that?'

When wanderers of other religions say this, you should say to them: 'Reverends, when the Buddha describes what's included in happiness, he's not just referring to pleasant feeling. The Realized One describes pleasure as included in happiness wherever it is found, and in whatever context."

Pañcakaṅgasutta- SN 36.19

Chapter 15:

Renunciation

Some people mistakenly believe that the joys of renunciation are achieved through painful ascetic practices and manipulating external factors. However, in the Buddha's path, renunciation is attained through understanding the pain experienced in one's life, awakening to the essence of life, and shaping one's mental states by applying wisdom. In that sense, you have to understand that there is nothing externally you have to do to experience Nibbana. You may choose you to have external factors as the way you want, and regardless of various external factor a person chose, it is the internal factors that contribute you to experience Nibbana.

It is important to understand that a person from any conventional background can become an Arahant; a king can be an Arahant. However, when a king becomes an Arahant, his mental state transforms, and he will no longer be interested in pursuing kingship unless engaging in royal duties helps in preserving and sharing the Dhamma. Therefore, the intentional actions of an Arahant will cease concerning worldly duties. However, they will continue when it comes to sharing the Dhamma, especially during times or occasions when true Arahants are rare. A person possessing higher knowledge across the four stages of Nirvana, and are not grasping ten fetters is a monk within the mental continuum regardless of conventional background.

Dhamma has significantly declined over the centuries, causing spiritual practitioners to lose the noble view. Practicing Dhamma means aligning with the universal Nirvana Dhamma and letting go of grasping at ten fetters. Due to the loss of the noble view and the practice aimed at experiencing the four stages of Nirvana Dhamma, many individuals in monastic settings do not practice as they should. When they fail to practice correctly or as the Buddha taught, no matter what they do, they cannot attain the fourfold Nibbana. This applies to any setting because the setting itself is not relevant for universal Nirvana Dhamma; rather, the training leading to the four stages of Nirvana Dhamma is what matters.

Dhamma has declined to the extent that these days, in general, people think that the Sangha on the noble path refers only to those wearing a particular dress code. However, the Sangha means being a Sotapanna,

Sakadagami, Anagami, or Arahant, regardless of what they wear. When people prioritize ordinary Sangha members, they will only gain ordinary Dhamma knowledge and merits what an ordinary person can offer to another. Ideally, Ordinary monks should confess their wrongdoings to the universal Sangha to make progress on the noble eightfold path.

Many people mistakenly think that painful ascetic practices are essential for achieving Nibbana. In truth, what is needed is an awakening to genuine life experiences that help reduce desires and greed for oneself. This awakening allows for a true cessation of cravings in the mind. Given that individuals have different mind states and circumstances, some people may choose to engage in ascetic practices if they believe these practices will help them reduce their desires. Others might avoid ascetic practices if they feel these practices are unsuitable for reasons such as health or other circumstances. Ultimately, what matters is not whether one employs ascetic practices or other external factors, but the effort one puts into shaping a mind free from greed, hatred, and deluded understanding. To do that what you should do is to reduce likes, dislikes, expectations within your daily life. This emphasizes that the path to Nibbana is the same for everyone. It involves letting go of the ten fetters or mental attachments and developing a mind that finds refuge in the universally applicable Triple Gem, rather than relying on conventionally limited Dhamma and Sangha.

Chapter 16:
Views

The word "enlightenment" is used by individuals from various spiritual paths to describe what they understand as enlightenment. Many spiritual traditions utilize the word enlightenment to explain their practices. Occasionally, people use the word in contexts outside of spirituality, such as naming a restaurant. That is to say, "enlightenment" is a term whose meaning, as taught by the Buddha, involves four stages. Nowadays, many people misinterpret the word "enlightenment" as merely a concept of Buddhism or a tradition. However, the four stages of Nirvana Dhamma are not merely conventions or constructs that people can invent like they do with various other subjects, or "Buddhism" as a concept or an academic discipline and similar ideologies. Instead, enlightenment across four stages of Nirvana Dhamma is an experience, a universal phenomenon, much like birth for sentient beings.

Views such as "I am here", "I am not here", "I am cosmos", "I am not cosmos" and the like should not be discussed, because talking about such things is meaningless for the purpose of Nibbana, Cessation. Given that the human life span is short, considering that there is only so much a person can do to experience four-fold Nibbana to extinguish sufferings, talking about irrelevant things is not helpful for those who seek a way out of mental pain. For example, if one has the view "I am here" and "I am not here", such a view cannot make one experience less mental pain, because mental pain comes from desires for self and for society/standard social practices and other fetters (desire to reborn, etc.). Thus, unless these fetters are let go across fourfold Nibbana, one cannot let go of mental pain with stability by merely talking about various views especially when these views are not directly related to Nibbana and are irrelevant. Talking about irrelevant things; such as various views that are not related to four-fold Nibbana, will be merely a waste of time and of a spiritual practice.

Out of compassion to people who seek escape from sufferings, Buddha did not encourage others to talk about things irrelevant to Dhamma and waste their precious time that's left out for them to practice in a way that leads to fourfold Nibbana. This also explains why noble precepts include not talking about irrelevant things at least during the time one allocates for one's spiritual practice.

Chapter 17:
The law of nature vs. social practices

Universal Dhamma and the four stages of Nirvana Dhamma operate at a universal level; they are not confined to the societal level. Things established at the societal level are often unstable. For example, all ordinations are temporary. Since everyone is subject to death, those who ordain and become conventional monks or nuns and householders will not remain in that status forever, but only for a short time. In contrast, those who attain Nirvana Dhamma across the four stages escape the cycle of birth and death, experiencing a stable Nirvana that transcends conventional existence. This highlights the importance of understanding Nirvana Dhamma as a transformative bond, reshaping conventions. This means a person's conventional background should not be a priority for following the noble path; rather, understanding the mental states of a person is relevant.

A person is experiencing the world by their thoughts of intentional actions that are grasping self-view and other fetters or karma. Karma is the law of consequences of intentional actions of beings who grasp fetters, a part of the universal truth. If you are merely looking at conventions and external features, you are using the wrong measures to understand who an Arahant is. Instead, you should focus on understanding a person's mind states.

It is important to explore the mind states of an individual to determine whether or not they have grasped the ten fetters, regardless of external conventions, physical characteristics (such as gender, age, caste, etc.), or mere words and actions that can be seen from the outside. Since intentional actions are a part of karma, you need to learn how to understand the intentional actions of others. This leads us to the question: how can an ordinary person analyze another person's mind states through specific intentional actions? This can be answered as follows:

Intentional actions of a person who is grasping their self-view and the ten fetters are creating new karma. Anyone who has relinquished the ten fetters is free from creating new karma or intentional actions. This means that to measure one's intentional actions, you need to assess the extent to which one has let go of grasping the ten fetters. This brings us to the next question: How can you measure one's extent of letting go of fetters in their mental states? By taking the fetters as indicators, you can gauge the degree of one's grasping of these fetters. For example, if you want to assess the extent of grasping related to self-view, you could ask the following questions: 1. How much does a person like to show off? 2. How much does a person like to boast about themselves? 3. How often does a person compare themselves to others with the intent to downgrade them? 4. How easy is it for a person to let go of past events/future events/represent events they have experienced or are experiencing? 5. To what extent can a person refrain from discussing topics that are not relevant to Dhamma during designated Dhamma discussions? Etc. Similarly, if you want to consider the extent of grasping in social practices, you might use the following questions to investigate mental states: 1. To what extent can you choose to do the right thing, thinking independently, despite what the majority thinks or says? 2. To what extent are you willing to become a good person, focusing on self-regard regardless of what others think, say, or do? This approach emphasizes that social practices are not perfect. To become a good person, you must often go beyond social norms and adhere to what is right in line with Dhamma. Let's say that in a particular society, people tend to become sad when they lose things or people often mistreat or marginalize a certain category of individuals or people kill animals during functions. However, in line with the Dhamma, one should not simply follow the customs that the majority adopts but go beyond standard social practices to apply Dhamma. That means instead of becoming sad when experiencing a loss, one might choose to remain indifferent. One might choose not to marginalize or mistreat anyone, despite the fact that certain categories of people are often mistreated in some societies. This approach encourages a focus on applying Dhamma within oneself rather than others, and a sense of self-responsibility for following Dhamma within. This is how a person can begin to cross the flood, independent of society and others which means renouncing the common way of doing things.

One interesting thing about practicing Dhamma is that generalization based on external factors should be avoided as each individual's mental state is unique and shaped by their thoughts experiencing the world coming from sensory experiences. Rather generalization based on categories of thoughts are a more reliable way in understand mind state and how mind state shape individual experiencing the world coming from sensory experiences.

Chapter 18:
Inner path for all

The path to Nibbana is the same for everyone. It involves letting go of the ten fetters or mental attachments and developing a mind that finds refuge in the universally applicable Triple Gem, rather than relying on conventionally limited Dhamma and Sangha.

For centuries, you have heard about how to change external circumstances, but rarely have you learned how to detox your thoughts from worldly toxins. If you come across insights that go beyond what you've heard before, it's an indication that you are encountering higher Dhamma, four-fold Nibbana which is rare to find. If you lead the spiritual life irrationally, you cannot win the fruit, regardless of whether you make a wish or not. But, if you lead the spiritual life rationally, you can win the fruit, regardless of whether you make a wish or not. When someone has a wrong view, and when they develop wrong speech and wrong mindfulness based on the wrong view, they cannot benefit or gain fruition out of Buddha's Dhamma. An ordinary unwise person can attend and be devoted to a similar person meaning to another ordinary unwise person.

Purity in one's mind allows one to see purity in another. Lack of wisdom in one's mind prevents one from seeing wisdom in another. An ordinary person who lacks wisdom is unable to comprehend noble people. On the other hand, an ordinary person with wisdom can comprehend universal Dhamma in the words of universal Sangha to a reasonable extent. This is because when someone speaks, another person can only understand from within their own understanding.

A person who has excessive greed, hate, and delusion struggles to comprehend someone who has lesser greed, hate, and delusion. They cannot imagine that such a state is possible for another person simply because they cannot experience those mind states themselves. This explains why some individuals with an ego misinterpret that only a person with ego can declare Arahantship. If we were to question how an Arahant can have an ego, we would see that it is impossible. Yet, people with an ego often make claims about Dhamma, concealing the fact that they lack understanding of the four stages of Nibbana due to a lack of integrity. On the other hand, true Arahants declare their experiences openly, taking full responsibility for their declarations. Declaring one's insights and taking responsibility is a noble quality in a person. Following the Buddha's footprint, Arahants do not declare Dhamma matters without disclosing their qualifications, and whatever they say, they express without ego. This is how you should comprehend the different mind states of human beings. A noble person with wisdom can comprehend in another's mind that they are greedy, they have hatred, are deluded, have wrong views and the like. Conversely, when a person has the right view and cultivates right speech and mindfulness based on that view, they can reap the benefits and achieve results from the Buddha's Dhamma. Therefore, by understanding what Nibbana is and recognizing the correct practices associated with it, one can develop Nibbana within themselves. Those who practice the Dhamma in accordance with the right view will have the opportunity to experience the fourfold Nibbana.

Chapter 19:

Fake Dhamma

The qualities of an unwise ordinary person are they are not loyal and devoted to Buddha, they make new versions of Dhamma that are imperfect in qualities, not caring, proud, and are unwise so they only know what society creates and presents. The qualities of a noble person are that they don't make new versions of Dhamma but know about four stages of Nirvana Dhamma through personal experience, are loyal and devoted to Buddha, for Buddha and Buddha's Dhamma allow people and gods to escape sufferings, the best thing of all and they don't grasp self-view, conventions and other fetters in mind. They don't misinterpret Dhamma, don't hurt self or another, are dutiful and responsible, are caring, are not proud, and are wise so that they know more than what society presents in the ways of how the universe functions. And how does an untrue person meaning unwise ordinary person have the intentions of an untrue person? It is when they present perfect universal Buddha and Dhamma as imperfect Buddha and Dhamma. This means a person's conventional background should not be a priority for following the noble path; rather, understanding the mental states of a person is relevant. This is how you should comprehend higher Dhamma and Sangha related matters.

Chapter 20:
Ego

Myths about universal Nibbana is that some ordinary people suggest that those who declare their qualifications should refrain from doing so because it may indicate a kind of ego or conceit. As discussed earlier, those who believe this often have their own ego and conceit, making it difficult for them to imagine how someone else could declare their qualifications without feeling the same ego and conceit.

Every individual can understand another person's mental state through their own experiences. When someone's mind is filled with excessive greed, they struggle to see purity in others, and what they say often reflects their own mental state. Yet, what is true is that Arahants do not have an ego. They share the higher Dhamma out of loving kindness without expecting anything for themselves. To understand their mind state, it is important to recognize that mind states vary among individuals. Additionally, the mind states differ between ordinary people and those who are noble. Furthermore, mind states evolve through the four stages of Nirvana Dhamma.

Chapter 21: Finding the true Dhamma

One way people find Nibbana is through accepted practices of Dhamma and by connecting with socially accepted practices. For a long time, you may have been honoring conventional Dhamma and the Sangha without questioning them whether or not they have experienced Nirvana Dhamma. However, you should move beyond these conventions. As you do, you will come to comprehend the universal experience of Nibbana. No matter how much they seek, many fail to find Nirvana within socially accepted interpretations of Dhamma and the conventional Sangha. This is because the experience of Nirvana is shaped by one's karma, merits, and wisdom.

There are two paths in the practice of Dhamma. One is the accepted way, which is easy to promote and has been taught for centuries. This path tends to attract many followers and often results in material gains and social recognition for the teacher and followers.

The other is the true Dhamma, which transcends conventional teachings. This path attracts only a small number of wise individuals and does not lead to material gains; instead, it offers the potential to enhance wisdom to expand pleasures derived from worldly experiences to experience Sotapanna state and end the cycle of samsara.

Those who follow the accepted versions of Dhamma may receive material support, respect, and honor, but they miss out on the blissful experience of Nibbana.

The truest path may require going against societal norms, embracing freedom from worldly life including material attachments, and attachment for social recognition and striving for total extinguishment of desires—the ultimate goal.

For centuries, we have seen ordinary Sangha inviting you to embrace the accepted version of Dhamma, and it often becomes a matter of mere following social practices and alike without awakening to the truth.

An alternative path is to seek the truth that goes beyond social practices, universal happening actively—investigating, applying, and testing what seems true—until one experiences Nibbana for oneself.

You may try and reflect on Dhamma and Sangha matters as follows;

In noble path, there are no unusual things to do, most things of Dhamma you need to apply within your daily activities. There is no need to conduct retreats or meditation classes to experience the Sotapanna state. The peace experienced during these events tends to be short-lived. Instead, learning to cultivate a peaceful mind in the midst of everyday life is a more realistic approach to awakening and truly experiencing life. However, for teachers who value material gains and honor, encouraging you to practice Dhamma independently means they would not receive regular fees and benefits from you. Consequently, some members of the Sangha, even if they understand that the practices they preach do not lead to Nibbana, continue to promote the same methods.

Sangha members who try to please you—by attending birthday parties, weddings, and various ceremonies—often seek to maintain goodwill to gain personal benefits. Alternatively, there are Sangha members who do not concern themselves with pleasing or displeasing anyone. They focus on presenting the truth and sharing worldly applicable insights. Even if they visit you or do not visit you personally, they guide you on how to awaken to a true life experience without treating Dhamma as a separate practice. They encourage you to integrate Dhamma into your daily routine and take personal responsibility to understand, shape, and enhance wisdom in your thoughts. This approach empowers you to reduce the mental pain you experience. These individuals do not expect anything from you or make you dependent on them; instead, they help you become an independent person capable of taking good care of your well-being and that of others.

Those who seek to please or displease you, making you dependent on them, are ordinary people or ordinary Sangha. In contrast, those who do not aim to please or displease but show you how to become fully capable and independent in caring for your own well-being and that of others, while explaining higher Dhamma to enhance your understanding and improve your mental state, are transcending ordinary practices. They embody the qualities of a noble Sangha.

This situation can be explained as follows: People like Devadatta use the word "Dhamma" or "Nirvana" and alike, but they do not represent true Dhamma. They aim to please and entertain you with various practices, such as retreats, meditations and similar activities, as it allows them to continue their practice and life style. These activities may provide you with temporary relief, but that's not what Buddha taught. Buddha did not teach a way to experience a temporary escape from worldly pain but rather a path to stable relief. To achieve this stable relief, you must learn to apply Dhamma day and night in regular life and not misunderstand that temporary comforts are ways of practicing for balanced mind states in your daily life. Instead of merely practicing ways of temporary relief, you must extend your practice of Dhamma during normal daily life by reducing the attachments that bind you to misguided sense of self, others and the world, including societal norms and practices. It is important to extend your Dhamma practice throughout your waking hours, regardless of whether you are walking, sitting, or lying down. You can reflect on higher Dhamma (i.e., letting go of grasping the fetters) while engaging in your usual daily activitics. This is something you can do on your own, as self-training is the best way to develop wisdom about self. In today's economy, where many people are facing difficulties and find it hard to access mental health support freely, you don't need to pay a fee to a teacher to improve your mind state and well-being. Instead, you can learn to empower yourself by learning to apply wisdom within your daily life.

"Others said, "Arahant Sāriputta has a unique way of coming and going; he seems independent and does not care much to please or displease us." But Devadatta is our constant companion, both on festival days and on ordinary days he comes to chat with us, and is ever ready like a water-pot, he come and spend time with us. Let us give it to him." After a long discussion it was decided by a majority of four to give the robe to Devadatta. So they gave the robe to Devadatta."

-Dhp 9 & 10

Extending happiness and peace derived from worldly pleasures to enhance your well-being is far more important than merely inviting you to practice that does not lead to experiencing Nibbana or participating in a ceremony or events. It is not easy for someone who is consumed by greed and desires for personal gain (such as money, material possessions, honor, or relationships that arise from following social standards) to teach about cessation and Nibbana, which transcend self-centeredness and provide a way out of it. This is because, when you go with the stream and follow the standard social practices, you can easily get social approval and the gains that comes with social approval such as materials, honours and the like. Yet, universal Nibbana goes beyond social practices. Those who speak of Dhamma as merely a convention are revealing an ordinary state of mind. Likewise, it is challenging for someone with a degree of ill will, based on a misguided understanding of self and the belief that conventional norms are stable, to teach about cessation or to free themselves from such concepts to experience Nibbana.

Nibbana goes beyond standard social practices and norms; one who represents it requires representing alone beyond the social settings. This explains why Buddha recommended Sangha to roam alone (see also, "wander alone like a rhinoseraus", Khaggavisana Sutta, *Sn 1.3*) without forming attachment for associates based on deluded understanding.

At rare occasions, you will meet individuals like Arahant Sariputta who do not associate with anyone based on likes, dislikes, or expectations, as they are free from such attachments based on deluded understanding that self and social practices are stable. They focus on explaining higher Dhamma to help you awaken and understand true life experiences. Given there are many people who present an incorrect version of Dhamma and Sangha, chances are that the majority of people are often deceived by untrue people who pretend to be true disciples of Buddha, like Devadatta. It is rare to find someone who can genuinely help you awaken to understand true life experiences, such as Arahant Sariputta. By reflecting on these words, you may develop a deeper understanding of how to enhance your mental states gradually over time across stages of Nibbana, keeping in mind what is best for your well-being. The path to experiencing Sotapanna involves reducing attachment to the first three fetters while associating with the Universal Triple Gem meaning appreciating and reflecting the qualities of the universal Triple Gem and developing noble virtues based on right view.

Someone who genuinely cares for and respects you wants to show you how to let go of a distorted understanding of yourself, others, and the world. This can lead to experiencing a stable peace and happiness that does not depend on external factors such as a dress code, appearance, or conventions that are subject to change or internal factors such as meditation practices, or jhanas that are subject to change. Instead, you may develop the right understanding of higher Dhamma that does not depend on external factors or internal factors to experience stable happiness and peace that does not depend on self, others and the world through four stages of nibbana.

"Not irritable or pretentious, not grasping precepts and observances, tamed, bearing their final body: that's who I call a perfected one...

Not deriving pleasure or have desire for mixing with or associating anyone (including friends, family, ordinary sangha and noble Sangha etc.); like a migrant with no shelter meaning living without grasping where one lives and not grasping others in one's mind, one who is not grasping desires (likes, dislikes, expectations): that's who I call a perfected one."

- Vāseṭṭhasutta, MN 98

To bridge the gap between conventional Dhamma and universal Dhamma, one must learn to renounce the grasping self-view and conventional beliefs. Nibbana is a gradual training process over four stages. Initially, one requires gaining Sotapanna. To experience the Sotapanna stage, you might initially enhance the wholesome aspects of your life by becoming a good person who is responsible for fulfilling your responsibilities to yourself and others. As you develop the joy of doing wholesome things, that joy can help you find inner peace. For example, when you respect and care for yourself, you might not want to cling to your painful thoughts or dwell on painful thoughts for the sake of your well-being. When you extend the same level of respect and care to everyone, you might not want to hurt anyone intentionally. When you respect those who have cared for you and appreciate those who have supported your growth, such as parents, teachers, you cultivate the good qualities of a person. When you extend the same level of respect and care to everyone, you nurture your own noble qualities. In this way, those who aspire to develop happiness and peace on the path of Buddha—leading to the Sotapanna state—should be able to find joy and tranquility in your noble thinking and behavior, even when your mind is experiencing an ordinary state along its mental continuum.

Furthermore, when you reflect on the qualities of the Buddha and the Arahants of all times, you should be able to experience joy and happiness in your mind from recalling their wisdom based virtuous qualities. This is how an ordinary person, an outsider disciple, can train to become an insider disciple on the noble path, which means Sotapanna and alike. In this way, you may continue to learn to increase joy, happiness, and peace by engaging in wholesome actions while reducing unwholesome thoughts, such as believing that what you like should dictate your happiness and alike.

Buddhahood is a state of wisdom, which involves developing an understanding of yourself, your thoughts, and your life experiences that goes beyond what your sensory information presents to you. There are six sensory organs, and wisdom is something that lies beyond these six senses. This is what you need to cultivate in order to follow the Buddha's path.

Chapter 22:
Nibbana and the human nature

Nibbana aligns with human nature. When individuals are born, they naturally have the underlying tendency to like or dislike worldly experiences from birth. Even among monastic communities, where the majority are ordinary people, there are many misunderstandings of higher Dhamma. These misunderstandings prevent them from developing the noble path. Therefore, it's important to clarify these misconceptions.

There are many training practices being promoted by ordinary people or the Sangha that claim to lead to the noble path. If any teachings have been introduced by someone other than the Buddha, they can hinder the noble path, as it diverges from the Buddha's teachings. Only the Buddha and his enlightened disciples truly understand this. When someone explains the Dhamma to another person, both the explainer and the recipient remain unaware until genuine understanding is achieved. This is why many people who have explained the Dhamma may still lack comprehension, resulting in followers who are also not knowledgeable about it. As a result, we find a multitude of individuals who are either unaware of or misconceiving universal Dhamma.

It is important to note that modern-day Vipassana meditations are not the Vipassana that the Buddha taught, nor are they equivalent to the jhana practices. Today, there are numerous practices that are not recommended by the Supreme Buddha. By adopting practices not introduced by Buddha himself, disciples in various countries continue to practice without achieving fruition. This highlights the importance of discussing the authentic path to Nirvana, which involves letting go of attachments and progressing through the four stages of universal Nirvana Dhamma.

One may live wherever is convenient and suitable according to one's choice, and becoming attached to where one lives is what causes suffering. Thus, describing practices based on external factors is the wrong approach; it is not a noble way to understand the Dharma. It is not merely about a person's lifestyle, ascetic practices, or leaving home to live in a monastery. These are basic practices known for outside disciples, but the noble practices lie beyond those commonly adopted by outside disciples. The reason can be explained as follows.

Liking or disliking something is a state of mind. Mind training is the same for all. The world is interpreted and understood through our thoughts. To cease to exist in the world requires training the mind. Nowadays, many meditation classes exist, but these practices are not sufficient to experience the four stages of Nirvana Dhamma. One reason for the growth of such non-dhamma practices is the greed, hatred, and delusion of those who call themselves Dharma teachers or sharers. They often lack integrity, telling you things that are not aligned with what you should actually practice. There is no remarkable difference in the mental states between bhikkhus, bhikkhunis, upasakas, and upasikas if they are grasping the fetters. This explains why during the Buddha's time, there were no strict status-based divisions between those who lived in monasteries and those who lived at home. Over time, some in monasteries began to desire status, material wealth, and honor, claiming to be the true sons of the Buddha, meaning disciples or followers of the Buddha. They suggested that those who live at home cannot become sons of the Buddha. This is a myth.

Nibbana is related to one's karma and merits, and is a universal experience. This means that a noble or universal Sangha can appear in any setting or from any background. Some have twisted the original Dhamma with the intention of elevating themselves, leading people who are not Sotapanna to believe that those who live in monasteries are the only noble ones. Over the centuries, as Dhamma declined, monasteries have propagated the idea that the Buddha's Dhamma means living as a monk in a monastic setting, which is misleading. Some practioners accept this without seeking the truth and merely accept things as they are. Yet, no amount of effort will make it so that only those who live in monasteries can become Arahants; this will not happen, despite the views of some misguided individuals.

It is human nature when you have something with which you are completely satisfied and are fulfilled, you no longer look for it. So, when an ordinary people transition into experiencing Sotapanna and Sakadagami states in their mental continuum, they naturally replace their sad, unhappy and unpleasant mind states to pleasure states wrapped in with sensual pleasures, a happening to them. They experience happiness 24/7, 365 days a year, regardless of circumstances. Happiness experienced by a Sotapanna is much more than an ordinary person can ever imagine; it's more like living in a heavenly state in a human body regardless of the circumstances. Having experienced maximum happiness beyond what an ordinary person can ever experience or imagine while still ordinary, when Sotapanna and Sakadagami continuously experience happiness wrapped in sensual pleasures beyond all happiness of worldly life, they become fully satisfied with it over time. Their need for happiness fulfilled, they are no longer looking for it, because their need for happiness becomes fully satisfied. Thereafter, at a later stage, having previously experienced endless happy states, a Sotapanna and Sakadagami will transit into experiencing "equanimity mind states" based on joy when recollecting the Triple Gem at a random time. At that point, a Sotapanna will give up happiness based on sensual pleasures to experience a different kind of joy and peace; a stable happiness by giving up sensual pleasures at the Anagami state.

Before Sotapanna, when you feel that there is too much pain in daily life and are interested and want to self-help to find a way out of pain which has no danger on the body or any harmful effects but are peaceful and blissful without hurting self or others, you should reflect on and apply Dhamma regularly (reflecting on impermanence, reducing pride, reducing likes, dislikes, not giving too much importance to social practices, listening to Dhamma talks, chants, engaging in Dhamma activities) to escape pain and seek friendship with noble persons of four kinds. This is the practice recommended to you by the Buddha to reach the noble path.

Chapter 23:
Outsiders, noble laity and noble monks

Those who wish to understand Nibbana should understand the following. The noble path goes beyond mere social practices and requires one to let go of grasping tendencies. You can learn to understand Dhamma and Sangha beyond conventional interpretations.

Some people give priority to relationships, family, and the like, which is also the doing of Sotapanna and Sakadagami. This explains why Sotapanna and Sakadagami are called lay people in the noble path.

Those who are not at least a Sotapanna are outsiders and are neither "lay people" or "monks" in Buddha's path. They are outsiders and not yet the disciples of the Buddha. This explains why all these years you hear the teachings of outsiders that are limited and imperfect, such as tradition, lifestyle, division and the like. When you hear Dhamma from outsiders, you hear outsiders' Dhamma and not the universal perfect Dhamma of the perfect Buddha known and shared by noble disciples who are either lay (meaning Sotapanna or Sakadagami) or monks (Anagami and

Arahants). Some ordinary people give priority to lifestyles, because their understanding is limited to lifestyles that are based on social practice, and their understanding is not universal Dhamma, Nibbana. Some ordinary people give priority to traditions, divisions and alike, because their understanding is limited to traditions, divisions and alike, and their understanding is not universal Dhamma, Nibbana.

Outsiders can explain only outsiders Dhamma, which can be recognized, because they always have limitations and are imperfect in qualities. The Buddha never recommended taking refuge in outsiders. This explains why, when outsiders such as conventional monks and conventional householders who are still training to becoming noble ones, they are not supposed to take refuges in the Bhikkhu Sangha but are supposed to take refuge in the universal noble Sangha. When true Dhamma in decline and true Sangha are rare to find, people misunderstood that someone living a lifestyle based on rituals and rules as disciples of the Buddha but you may correct your misunderstanding to understand universal Dhamma.

There are many subtle things about Dhamma that an ordinary person may not comprehend well enough to develop a practice. Yet, by understanding these subtle things about Dhamma, a wise person can develop the right understanding of Dhamma.

The noble path is based on the right understanding of Dhamma. To develop higher Dhamma that goes beyond social practices meaning Nibbana across four stages, you should understand who are outsiders and insiders ("lay people" and "monks") in the noble path as interpreted by the Buddha (Please note that words such as "insiders", "outsiders", and "lay people or monks" in the noble path are merely used to explain higher Dhamma but not to treat people differently, or treat anyone as superior, same, or inferior to another. This is because the purpose of noble friendship is to share higher wisdom, and higher Dhamma knowledge across four stages and merits without grasping self-view and other fetters.

"Venerable sir, what is the reason, what is the cause, why formerly there were fewer conventional Sangha but more noble Sangha coming from various backgrounds, while now there are more conventional Sangha but fewer noble disciples and Arahants who are established in final knowledge?"

When beings are deteriorating in Dhamma practice and the true Dhamma and true Sangha are disappearing there are more conventional Sangha but few noble Sangha coming from various backgrounds. Kassapa, the true Dhamma does not disappear so long as a counterfeit of the true Dhamma has not arisen in the world. But when a counterfeit of the true Dhamma arises in the world, then the true Dhamma disappears..."

- Saddhammappatirūpakasutta, SN 16.13

"...Someone who totally and utterly lacks these four factors of stream-entry is an outsider who belongs with the ordinary persons..."

(i.e. Regardless of whether a person is ordained or not based on social practices, one is an outsider until one experience stream entry in the words of the universal Buddha) -Nandiyasakkasutta, SN 55.40

With regard to today's context, almost everyone in monastic settings and non-monastic settings are lay persons because anyone who has not experienced the Anagami state is a lay person who possesses an underlying tendency for sensual desires that come from sensory experiences.

Interpreting Sangha through conventional perspectives does not align with the noble path. Therefore, when you understand Dhamma and Sangha based on conventions, you are adopting an ordinary view rather than the right view of the noble path. Regardless of these conventions, you can learn to comprehend the universal Sangha through states of mind that are not bound by ten fetters.

This is not to discriminate but simply to clarify Dhamma. Those who let go of grasping outsider's perspective are developing Dhamma vision leading to Sotapanna.

By practicing in the right way, one may develop one's understanding and right speech, right efforts that are based on right understanding to experience Sotapanna, Sakadagami, Anagami and Arahant states of Nibbana.

Chapter 24: Renunciation

There are many myths about Nibbana. These myths can prevent spiritual friends from understanding the higher Dhamma, and for that reason, it's worth discussing some of the misconceptions surrounding the four stages of Nibbana.

For a long time, people have misinterpreted the characteristics of a perfected renunciant by focusing on external appearances or external factors and conventions. Instead, one should seek individuals who have genuinely given up worldly desires in mind, regardless of their outward circumstances. The characteristics of a perfected renunciant include: - They do not grasp worldly experiences. - They have relinquished ten fetters. - They are awakened to the true nature of life. - They do not become sorrow by worldly experiences. - They harbor no ill will, and do not regard anyone as better than another or divide people with the intent to downgrade others. - They do not pretend or act insincerely. - They possess naturally occurring noble qualities. - They have finalized their existence in samsara and will not be reborn. - They have given up sensual pleasures. - They understand for themselves the end of suffering. - They possess deep wisdom that goes beyond ordinary understanding. - They know what constitutes the training path to becoming a Sotapanna (stream-enterer) and what does not. - They use possessions without attachment. - They are free from greed, hatred, and conceit, and consider others as precious. - They have no expectations; they act without seeking anything in return- They understand the rebirth of beings and have attained liberation from the cycle of rebirth. - They possess triple knowledges and likewise.

One is not a perfected one by birth, rituals, precepts or standard social practices. One is a perfected one by not grasping the ten fetters, and intentional actions that are free from grasping the fetters.

Chapter 25: Praise vs downgrade

You may have noticed that some members of the ordinary Sangha praise living a monastic lifestyle as a pathway to becoming a son or direct disciple of the Buddha. This is a misconception because the training path to universal Nirvana doesn't involve changing external factors but rather developing wisdom and merits within.

When someone claims that a person living in a monastery is a monk who is aligned with the noble path, it is either a misunderstanding of universal Nirvana Dhamma or a misrepresentation of the Buddha's teachings. This could stem from ignorance or a deliberate attempt to deceive for the sake of self-praise. In either case, someone who deliberately lies or praises themselves is not adhering to the true essence of practice, regardless of whether they live in monastic or non-monastic settings. Self-praise and belittling others go against the practice of the universal noble path. These behaviors indicate an attachment to the worldly existence. Instead, one can use a monastic setting to accurately interpret the Dhamma and speak the truth.

So, how does the Sangha contribute to the elimination of the Buddha's Dhamma? By engaging in actions not recommended by the Buddha, knowingly or unknowingly, some ordinary Sangha members can contribute to the dilution or elimination of universal Dhamma.

To attain the state of Sotapanna in mind, there is a unified training path that applies to everyone, regardless of their setting. What is truly needed are noble virtues grounded in the right view, which are universally applicable. You may focus more attention on developing the right view by reducing grasping the fetters in mind and taking refuge in the universal Triple Gem.

Some individuals in a monastic setting may often praise the rules of monastic life and their commitment to following them. They do so because they praise one way of life, and that is misinterpreting Dhamma. A person can be a king, teacher, doctor, cleaner, carpenter, homeless individual, drunkard, or monk, depending on social standards; however, they all share the same fundamental training path: reducing attachment and the ten fetters rooted in a deluded understanding of the self and conventions are stable. When you correct your deluded understanding, you strengthen your right understanding of self, others, and the world. To let off a deluded understanding of self and the world, it's important to observe your mind and check if you notice any thoughts (i.e., you identify as feelings) such as excessive sadness, anxiety, worries, conceit, and similar things in your mind. If you do, try to reduce grasping the thoughts of excessive sadness, anxiety, worries, conceit and similar things, conceit and avoid making comparisons. When explaining Dhamma to someone else, focus on conveying the Dhamma as the Buddha intended. If you are uncertain about any aspect, acknowledge your uncertainty instead of misinterpreting the Dhamma or grasping conventions or limited Dhamma.

The right view refers to an accurate understanding of the four stages of Nibbana. Without this understanding, practitioners may become confused and feel lost, making it difficult for them to experience the bliss of Nibbana. The noble Sangha plays a crucial role in the universally applicable noble path by sharing the training with the community, allowing everyone to benefit from the practice. This raises an important reflection: many people today place excessive respect or fear on ordinary individuals in monastic settings solely based on their external appearance. This tendency can lead those in monastic life to continue their practices without the proper perspective, concealing their true mental states beneath their robes instead of working to purify their minds. Moreover, they may explain Nibbana and the practice incorrectly, preventing many from truly experiencing Nibbana. This is detrimental not only to themselves but also to their followers and the Sangha as a whole. An unrefined mind prolongs mental suffering and hinders the attainment of the benefits of spiritual practice, regardless of the environment. Instead, for the sake of purifying Dhamma and the Sangha, and for mutual assistance in overcoming shortcomings, may all members of the Sangha commit to understanding each other's mental states. May all members of the Sangha support one another in overcoming wrong views and failures in their spiritual practice, helping each other to develop the right view on the noble path. May spiritual communities unite and support one another with good intentions and kindness in letting go of attachments. This will enable them to experience the blissful state of Nibbana, which enhances both the quality of mind and the quality of life, ultimately leading to the end of samsara. In this way, the Sangha can open the noble doors that were made accessible to all by the Supreme Buddha, allowing many individuals the opportunity to experience the blissful state of Nibbana through joyful renunciation.

Individuals filled with excessive greed, hatred, and delusion can distort the Dhamma or even cause it to fade away. This explains why, in modern contexts, someone who truly attains Nibbana may choose not to join a monastic community. If an Arahant joins a monastery, it could inadvertently hinder others' paths to Nibbana, as some may mistakenly believe that an Arahant must live in a monastic setting, Nibbana is merely a life style or a tradition. This misconception could prevent the development of their right vision. True Arahants show respect for the universal Buddha and universal Dhamma through their solitary mind state meaning mind without attachment to self, others and the world regardless of whether they live in a monastic or non-monastic environment. This is because Nibbana goes beyond standard social practices and norms; one who represents it requires representing alone beyond the social settings. This explains why Buddha recommended Sangha to roam alone (see also, "wander alone like a rhinoseraus", Khaggavisana Sutta, *Sn 1.3*) without forming attachment for associates based on deluded understanding. While conventional differences exist to help people understand the basics of universal Dharma, it is essential to lessen attachment to conventions to experience the universal Dhamma.

Nibbana provides what many individuals seek in life: quality of mind and quality of life (and end to Samsara). Ordinary Sangha or the outsider disciples who attempt to represent the Triple Gem should develop their minds to let go of grasping the fetters through efforts. While practicing, you will have failures and setbacks. By making extra efforts to mend failures, grasping self-view and the fetters, one may continue a practice to progress into Sotapanna. Once after gaining Sotapanna, a person cannot fall back. After having experienced Anagami state and Arahantship, you can confirm the path leading to Nibbana with confidence, and it surely ends Samsara.

While many people today may not be familiar with fourfold Nibbana, they might mistakenly believe that Sotapannas, Sakadagamis, Anagamis and Arahants can only be found in monastic settings. In reality, they can be found in various contexts, among the rich and poor, educated and uneducated, including street cleaners and shop owners etc. This indicates that ordinary Sangh's understanding of Nibbana needs to evolve in today's society.

Every word spoken by the Buddha should not be wasted or ignored, as they are precious teachings. It's important to recognize that karma plays a significant role in Nibbana, and this is worth keeping in mind. Anyone who attains Nibbana should offer support and assistance to others without discrimination, valuing each member of Sangha community's contribution. They should encourage others to continue their development with good intentions, genuine care, and loving-kindness. It is important for them to share the wisdom that alleviates all suffering—a gift from the Supreme Buddha to the entire community of Sangha.

Chapter 26:
Wisdom and merits-based noble path

When one person who does not understand Nibbana through personal experience explains something to another, if neither fully understands the Dhamma, both remain in ignorance and fail to grasp the subject matter. This illustrates why, even when several people explain Dhamma without a proper understanding of higher Dhamma; Sotapanna, Sakadagami, Anagami, Arahant, they do not help those who follow them to know the Dhamma correctly. As a result, we have many individuals who either do not know or misunderstand the universal Dhamma.

Today, spiritual practitioners often adopt various practices that are either not recommended or differ from the teachings of the Supreme Buddha. It is important to note that modern-day Vipassana meditations are not the same as the Vipassana outlined in the four stages of universal Dhamma taught by the Buddha. Similarly, contemporary jhana practice differs significantly from the jhana that occurs naturally at the Anagami state and does not align with original practices. By following practices not introduced by the Buddha, many practitioners continue without achieving fruition.

The Buddha recommended a practice with four stages: Sotapanna, Sakadagami, Anagami, and Arahant. Therefore, it is essential to discuss the path to the four stages of universal Nirvana Dhamma, beginning with the training path to Sotapanna.

The path to Nirvana requires transcending self-view and letting go of attachments to conventions based on an illusory understanding of their stability as a whole. It involves taking refuge in the supreme Triple Gem. Taking refuge in the Triple Gem means more than merely uttering the words "I take refuge in the Universal Buddha, Dhamma, and Sangha." It entails understanding the universal significance of the Triple Gem. This is why the noble path begins with the right view of the universal Triple Gem and its aspects.

Speaking the truth, today among monastic communities, where the majority are ordinary people, there are many misunderstandings of higher Dhamma. These misunderstandings have obstructed their opportunity to develop along the noble path. Additionally, limited understanding of higher Dhamma has prevented followers of various monastic communities from developing the right view in the noble path. Therefore, it's important to clarify these misconceptions. When it comes to the noble path, one common misconception is that a monk is someone who attains monkhood solely through social ordination. A person who receives monkhood through this conventional process is known as a conventional monk. However, a true monk or inner disciple of the Buddha goes beyond conventions to experience the four stages of universal Nirvana Dhamma, which are: Sotapanna, Sakadagami, Anagami, and Arahant.

In universal Dhamma practice, particularly in the pursuit of the fourfold universal Nirvana Dhamma, there is a practice of honouring the "wisdom and merits order", where individuals show respect to those who possess wisdom and inner qualities greater than their own. The Buddha stands at the top of this merits order, as there is no one above him, which means he does not need to respect anyone else. Similarly, Arahants, who have attained a high level of realization do not need to respect anyone else for the purpose of receiving wisdom and merits to experience fourfold Nirvana Dhamma, with the universal Buddha being their only superior in the order of merits.

This respect within the "wisdom and merits order" is intended for trainees (Sotapanna, Sakadagami, Anagami and outsider disciples or ordinary Sangha) to cultivate wisdom and merits, rather than Arahants seeking respect for themselves. In reality, you would see the Buddha and Arahants functioning without seeking respect in their daily lives, meaning they respect others and care for them without wanting respect for themselves. On the noble path, for Arahants, the purpose is not to receive respect but to help others eliminate suffering. If respecting others aids in alleviating their suffering, that is more important. This is how you should understand the mindset of the Buddha and Arahants.

You may adopt the practice of reflecting on the four noble truths in daily life. When faced with life's difficulties, remember the Dhamma—reflect and understand that challenges are a part of life. Suffering or mental distress is a natural part of existence. Recognize with wisdom that worrying excessively about these challenges is futile. The root of worry often lies in the expectations you have—that such challenges should not occur, or in your dislike for these experiences. Suffering arises from these expectations based on a deluded understanding that things are stable. To cease suffering, let go of this deluded understanding; relinquish your likes, dislikes, and expectations based on sensory experiences, which are inherently unstable. The path to cessation of suffering, or Nirvana, consists of four stages. The journey to becoming a Sotapanna requires reducing attachment to self-view, conventions, and doubts while taking refuge in the universal Triple Gem. In addition, you may maintain noble virtues as much as possible and engage in wholesome deeds.

Chapter 27:
Various practices and malpractices

Practitioners adopt different practices. By practicing in the right way, you will become free from sufferings coming from self and the world.

You may try to distinguish the difference between imperfect Dhamma and perfect Dhamma to differentiate what is non-Dhamma and what is the universal Buddha's perfect Dhamma. Everyone dies, but if someone divides people based on conventions and claims that innocent individuals (Upasaka) who have completed their training (Arahantship) will face death within 24 hours or 7 days, that is an imperfect interpretation of the Dhamma. This misinterpretation misrepresents the perfect and universal teachings of the Buddha. For example, when Nagasena, an ordinary monk, claimed that one who experiences Arahantship cannot survive more than seven days outside of a monastic context, this claim contradicts the perfect Buddha's perfect Dhamma. If the consequence of following imperfect Dhamma brings death for "Upasaka", the same does not apply to Buddha's perfect Dhamma. One who experiences Arahantship is no longer an "Upasaka" but a monk in words of Buddha because monk is a mental state in the noble path.

A sensible person should be cautious not to follow imperfect Dhamma. It is not recommended to follow an imperfect Dhamma for the sake of your well-being. Instead, you may follow Buddha's perfect Dhamma. One thing you must understand and remember is that the universal Buddha is the perfect among all perfected ones. The basic thing about Nibbana is that monastic lifestyle is not relevant for gaining fourfold Nibbana. Some monastic holders, who promote themselves as the disciples of the Buddha, completely ignore the words of Buddha. If the Buddha or Dhamma you know have imperfect qualities, they are fake and not genuine; the version of Buddha or Dhamma you know is not true Buddha or Dhamma.

To let go of your mental pain through four-fold Nibbana, you may grow your vision to understand perfect qualities of the universal Buddha and Dhamma. When you want to seek universal Dhamma, try to spot the difference between fake and the real version of universal Dhamma. When seeking universal Dhamma, try to look for perfect qualities in Dhamma. For example, if you were to think dana is a must to gain Nibbana, in that case, people who have less resources or no resources to offer dana can be prevented from Nibbana. Preventing some people simply because of their affluence is not ethical for perfect Dhamma. On many occasions, people gain Nibbana without offering anything but merely feeling grateful (see Matatakundali Vattu, Dhp 2) and appreciating Buddha, Dhamma and Sangha in their minds. Thus, one's wealth or material is not related to Nibbana but to one's wealth in thoughts, meaning that the extent to which you appreciate, reflect, and honour perfect qualities in universal Triple Gem is what allows you to develop higher merits. This explains why it is recommended to reflect on the qualities of the Triple Gem in thought.

Chapter 28:
Know the differences

As you can see in the path to Nirvana Dhamma, many aspects of life experience need to be understood. This explains why people who are literate can attain Nirvana Dhamma. Nowadays, there are many Buddhist scholars, yet even as a scholar, if you do not understand your life experience with wisdom, you are still likely to experience mental distress when faced with bad experiences in life which is a part of life for all. No amount of scholarly knowledge can help you reduce the mental distress that arises from life. That is not to say that becoming a scholar is not worthwhile, a personal choice; you may pursue scholarship if you wish. Yet, if you want to reduce pain and suffering in samsara, try and reduce likes, dislikes and expectations for your world created through sensory information. That is to say route to scholarship is one thing, route to becoming Sotapanna is another.

The path to the noble way is not the same as the conventional route taken by monks, which involves receiving ordination or permission from socially recognized monks or nuns. Instead, the noble path requires purifying one's thoughts to reflect the qualities of the universal Buddha, universal Dhamma and universal Sangha. By purifying your thoughts in this manner while reducing attachment to the fetters, one can experience Sotapanna within one's mental continuum.

Embracing the teachings that lead to Nirvana Dhamma is crucial, as the practice of universal Nirvana Dhamma remains the same for everyone.

Chapter 29: Beyond conceptual understanding and jhanas

Some spiritual practitioners discuss concepts. For instance, the phrase "I am cosmos" serves as a conceptual expression of one's being as part of the universe. However, a conceptual approach to enlightenment tends to result only in a conceptual understanding and does not necessarily alleviate mental suffering. For example, some practitioners may understand Buddha's Dhamma as a concept of interbeing, yet regardless of this understanding, they continue to maintain divisions within beings. This leads to desires that bind them to samsara. Let's say someone comes to a monastery and adopts the lifestyle of a monk. Regardless of where they live, they continue to exist bound by their understanding and misconceptions.

Ideally, spiritual practitioners seeking progress should recognize that views such as "I am here," "I am not here," "I am cosmos," "I am not cosmos," "idea of interbeing," "Buddha-nature," or "emptiness" are insufficient on their own. Practically implementing the idea of Buddha-nature is essential because merely discussing these concepts is meaningless in the pursuit of Nibbana, or cessation. Additionally, this highlights why noble virtues include the precept of avoiding meaningless conversations. Discussions about whether the cosmos is eternal or whether the soul and body are the same or different are not relevant to alleviating the mental pain a person experiences in daily life. Instead, the focus should be on enhancing the quality of the mind, life, and ultimately breaking free from samsara.

Other spiritual traditions emphasize the importance of focusing and developing concentration as a means to achieve enlightenment, often through practices like jhanas. However, concentration-based enlightenment yields experiences that are temporary and not eternal. While concentration helps the mind to focus and exist, such states eventually come to an end. Consequently, some people mistakenly believe they have attained Nirvana by following incorrect methods, such as focusing solely on jhanas. For them, there is rebirth, old age, death, and the presence of sorrow, lamentation, pain, sadness, and distress. I advocate for overcoming these challenges in this very life.

Since Dhamma alleviates suffering, both the Buddha and Dhamma are invaluable. Engaging in conversations about matters unrelated to the noble path not only wastes time but can also mislead people. This illustrates why the Buddha chose not to declare or participate in discussions about subjects unrelated to Nibbana. Additionally, it underscores why noble virtues include the precept of avoiding meaningless conversations. For example, discussing whether the cosmos is eternal or not, and whether the soul and body are the same or different, are topics that are not relevant to letting go of the mental pain a person experiences in daily life. Instead, the focus should be on enhancing the quality of the mind, life and ending samsara.

Depending on the chosen path of enlightenment, the outcomes can vary for those seeking Nibbana. The Buddha's path to enlightenment is developed through an understanding of life experiences with wisdom, leading to an awakening to true life experiences. To avoid misunderstanding and to shape understanding correctly, it is important to recognize that among those who believe they are following the Buddha's path but are not, there are individuals who develop jhanas through conscious concentration. This means they achieve concentration through deliberate efforts. However, in the Buddha's path, access concentration arises naturally once a person's mental continuum transforms into a noble state of mind, where no conscious effort is needed to experience jhanas.

Awakening to true life experiences through wisdom must be developed in alignment with the universal rhythm. This requires conscious effort to reduce fetters and associate with the noble order. As a result, transformation within a person's mental continuum leads to a mind that is free from suffering caused by the self, social practices, doubt, ill will, sensual desires, and cravings for form, etc. all in a stable manner.

Chapter 30: The easiest way

Ordinary people often discuss Dhamma loosely without making meaningful connections across the stages of Nirvana. This results in a superficial understanding; some individuals focus on one aspect, while others pick random aspects. Instead, it is important to see how the Dhamma leads to the four stages of Nirvana, as each stage is interconnected. Each aspect of the training path is linked to another, so there should be accuracy in understanding how these elements relate to one another across the stages of Nirvana. In this manner, first, you should focus on how a person explains Dhamma to understand who truly represent the Buddha.

"It is impossible, it cannot happen, for a stream entrant to divide the community of Sangha"-AN 1.268

One way to recognize a Sotapanna is that they do not divide the universal teachings. In other words, anyone who explains the Buddha's Dhamma as a tradition, division, or lifestyle may indicate that they do not truly understand Nirvana in depth because they lack personal experience. In other words, you should learn the essence of the noble Dhamma and find out to what extent a person explains universal Nirvana in line with the words of the Buddha.

One way to recognize an Arahant is to say that they know Buddha is the knower of all through personal experience:

"This, brahmin, is what is called 'a footprint of the Realized One' and also 'a trace of the Realized One' and also 'a mark of the Realized One'. At this point a noble disciple has not yet come to a conclusion, but they are coming to the conclusion., 'The Blessed One is a fully awakened Buddha...."

-Cūḷahatthipadopamasutta, MN 27

The easiest way to understand noble Sangha is to focus on how someone explains Dhamma matters and see how they present Dhamma as a happening beyond conventions, free from grasping fetters. You may learn to interpret the Dhamma and Sangha beyond conventional understanding.

Chapter 31:
Misunderstanding of the noble path

Some people claim that Nibbana can only be exclusively experienced by a particular group of individuals. This belief stems from the idea that Nibbana is a social phenomenon, overlooking the significant role that karma plays in attaining it. They may need to correct their understanding, as karma does not consider social aspects; rather, anyone who has practiced in the right manner can experience the benefits of Nibbana, shaped by their own karma. Although an ordinary person may not comprehend karma and rebirth fully, they can hear the confirmation of such things as true from those Arahants who have developed triple knowledge. If you try to apply the practice that is described by such Arahants, you should be able to test your truth and accept what you are told only when truth revealed to you.

Some people make statements that are incorrect, meaning statements that do not align with the views of noble individuals. The world is created within, and in the same way, Nibbana is also created within. The practice leading to Sotapanna involves reducing self-view and conventions while purifying through reflecting on the universal Triple Gem.

One common misconception made by ordinary people is the suggestion that those living in monastic settings should not declare their attainment of Nibbana to lay people. This claim is inaccurate and contradicts the Buddha's teachings of Dhamma. Firstly, most individuals in monastic settings are lay people on the noble path, meaning they have not completely relinquished the fetters of sensuality associated with the Anagami state. They remain outsiders (and not even the lay people in noble path; Sotapanna, Sakadagami) in their mental continuum, regardless of external factors. What should be emphasized instead is that anyone who genuinely attains Nibbana may share their insights with others, regardless of their conventional background. However, those who have not truly attained Nibbana should avoid making such claims, as this could mislead others and obstruct their path to Nibbana. This principle applies to all members of the Sangha, both monastic and non-monastic, not just a specific group.

Another misguided belief is that when a person declares their attainment of Nibbana, they feel pride. This perception reflects how some of the ordinary individuals misunderstand the mental state of true Arahants. Pride is characteristic of those who grasp onto self-view, which is subject to individual differences. In contrast, the mental state of an Arahant when they declare their Arahantship they don't feel pride. Imagine a good doctor in a hospital. When you encounter a qualified doctor, you appreciate their expertise not because they flaunt their qualifications, but because they genuinely want to help you recover out of care and compassion. This is true even though they are paid for their services and are just ordinary people. Therefore, consider the mind state of an Arahant who has relinquished all fetters when they declare their attainment; it is rooted in genuine compassion and the wish to assist others, rather than a desire to show off or seek praise or out of pride.

Thus, those who aspire to Nibbana and the good things in life and after for themselves may consider giving gifts in ten ways. The symbolic representation of ordinary bhikkhu is merely to help you remember the noble ones because noble ones are rare. Yet, the danger comes when you take the symbols as real, which is because both you and the ordinary bhikkhu will lose an opportunity to develop the noble vision and higher merits. Thus, those practitioners or if you were to take a stand against the words of the supreme Buddha where Dhamma lies beyond standard social practices (Nibbana is a universal law) by taking an ordinary monk as a noble one can hurt you and the ordinary bhikkhu in non-dhamma ways. Instead, by hearing the higher Dhamma, both you and the ordinary bhikkhu may develop towards extinguishment as it is meaningless to divide beings or maintain conceit in a path that leads to extinguishment for all.

In this way, each person's practice towards the noble path should only be used for extinguishment and not grasping. Each person's practice should only be used for not hurting self or others.

Chapter 32:
Wrong view of Dhamma

In general, the vast majority of spiritual practitioners don't interpret Buddha's Dhamma as interpreted by the Buddha, instead, they interpret Dhamma based on standard social practices because they have the vision of outsiders. Those who aspire to freedom from pain, Nibbana, would benefit, if they try and attempt to interpret Dhamma as interpreted by the Buddha. This will aid them in becoming a Sotapanna. As explained by Buddha, lay life, which means delight in worldly life, means liking, disliking, and expecting worldly experiences coming from sensory information.

Interpreting Dhamma and Sangha matters based on conventions is an ordinary way. However, interpreting Dhamma and Sangha matters from a perspective that goes beyond conventions is to enter the path of the noble ones, which goes against the stream. "Stream" refers to conventional ways of interpreting things and social practices. The noble path lies beyond conventions. When you understand things beyond conventions, you gain insight into how the universe works and grasp universal truths.

Birth and death are integral parts of how the universe functions. The universe is like a wave; it both gives and takes, and everything is subject to change. Therefore, if you apply wisdom to understand your life experiences, it will become clear that there is no reason to cling to things that are not stable. By reflecting on the impermanent nature of yourself, others, and the world around you, you can reduce feelings of sadness, anxiety, pride, jealousy, stinginess, and similar emotions. Additionally, this understanding helps you avoid dividing people based on social identities and treating them differently.

Understanding truth is a process that occurs through thoughts that are constantly flowing; it does not remain stable in the mind of an ordinary person. However, if you can reduce your attachment to a fixed self-view and social practices, and if you shape your thoughts, words, and actions with right mindfulness meaning wisdom to understand beyond conventions day and night while reflecting on the qualities of the Triple Gem that are universal and associating noble friends, this practice can lead you to experience blissful mind state across the fourfold Nibbana if you truly seek it.

The practice is merely a training in mind. The practice remains the same for all. The right practice and its strength will help you experience the stages of Nibbana within the shortest possible time.

Among those who believe they are following the Buddha's path but are not, there are those who develop jhanas through conscious concentration. This means they achieve concentration through deliberate efforts. However, in the Buddha's path, access concentration arises naturally after a person's mental continuum transforms into a noble mind state, where no conscious effort is needed to experience jhanas.

Besides, not everyone can understand the ways of karma works. It is only after hearing the words of Dhamma universally applicable to life experience that a person can recognize the wisdom that lies within Dhamma. Buddhahood is a state of wisdom. Wise words in a random person whose conceit is absent and has given up grasping conventions.

There are two categories of disciples: outsiders and insiders. Outsider disciples include ordinary monks, ordinary nuns, and male and female householders. They are bound to samsara as they cling to ten fetters. Insiders, on the other hand, have transcended conventional limitations and include the Sotapanna, Sakadagami, Anagami, and Arahant. In the context of the noble path, the term "lay" refers to Sotapanna and Sakadagamis. In this path, the term "monk" specifically refers to Arahants.

In ordinary terms, "monk" can refer to anyone who receives social ordination. In the noble path, "monk" denotes someone who has completed universal ordination shaped by karma and merits that ultimately ends birth, death, and the cycle of samsara regardless of external factors. If you can learn to understand and interpret the matters of Dhamma and Sangha in line with the noble path, you can develop the right vicw. By cultivating the right view, they can make progress on the noble path.

Chapter 33:
Giving up desire

Taking pleasure in wherever it is experienced is a reason for rebirth and sufferings.

This explains why it is important to train the mind not to take pleasures with deluded understanding across fourfold Nibbana. Experiencing pleasures coming from sensory information is one thing. Having a deluded understanding that pleasures can last long is another thing. What needs to be addressed is the latter, which simply reduces deluded understanding by broadening the vision on the way toward the noble path.

In general, one cannot extinguish desires at once. One cannot let go of deluded understanding instantly. There are four stages across which one can progress to perfect renunciation of desires.

Initially, one abandons sufferings only to experience pleasures at the Sotapanna stage.

Thereafter, one abandons the sense of pleasure at the Anagami stage.

Thereafter, one abandons desires for rebirth and such like at the Arahant stage.

Associating with noble ones helps you develop the noble vision.

Some people even make up new versions and their own versions of Dhamma and Sangha. These made-up versions of Dhamma and Sangha prevent you from reaching Nibbana.

Some people can follow a spiritual life ignoring the training, doing things that are not described by Buddha. One who aspires developing the noble vision must understand that a ritualistic life style is not relevant for developing the noble path, as rituals can be followed without necessarily letting go of self-view and conventions and reducing likes and dislikes, while living a ritualistic lifestyle. Regardless of what rituals a person follows or does not follow, letting go of self-view and conventions and reducing likes and dislikes will allow you to escape from the pain that self and society bring to you. While living in a monastic setting, one may develop the mind to let go of these things. The same is applicable for everyone.

Freedom gained from self, social practices and other fetters based on noble wisdom and noble qualities can be found in four categories of people: Sotapanna, Sakadagami, Anagami and Arahant.

When you appreciate something, it inspires you to develop similar wisdom and qualities within. You appreciate what you can develop within. Thus, appreciating a lot, meaning honouring someone for giving up the fetters in your thoughts, makes it possible for you to develop similar qualities within.

One's wealth or material is not related to Nibbana but to one's wealth in thoughts, meaning that the extent to which you appreciate, reflect, and honour perfect qualities in universal Triple Gem is what allows you to develop higher wisdom and merits. This explains why it is recommended to reflect on the qualities of the Triple Gem in thought.

Chapter 34:
Strict lifestyle vs noble path

One common myth is that a "monk" refers only to a conventional monk following the noble path. This is a misconception. It is important to understand that conventions and universal Nirvana function asynchronously. Conventions should merely be used to train the mind to a state that transcends grasping these conventions. This illustrates that all conventions serve as preliminary practices before reaching Sotapanna (stream-entry).

How can one use conventions to experience Sotapanna? The practice includes letting go of grasping fetters and renouncing attachments within daily life while forming a companionship with the universal Triple Gem.

An ascetic lifestyle is not the sole practice of Dhamma; rather, practicing Dhamma within any lifestyle is what defines a noble lifestyle. In other words, whether one lives an ascetic lifestyle or not, both must engage in the same training of the mind: letting go of attachments while taking refuge in the universal Triple Gem.

Practicing Dhamma means developing noble wisdom to let go of grasping the fetters while developing noble qualities within.

Nibbana addresses human nature. Human beings inherently have needs, some of which are basic. These include food to satisfy hunger, water to quench thirst, and the pursuit of happiness and peace from worldly distress in daily life—experiences they can enjoy while alive, without having to wait until after death or step outside their usual routine activities. Nibbana offers an escape from worldly distress and mental suffering, allowing individuals to find relief within their daily routines while still alive. This understanding reflects the perfect quality of the Buddha's universal Dhamma.

Nature is designed in such a way that food can satisfy hunger temporary, but it does not eliminate the need to eat again, and water can quench thirst only for a short time before the need arises again. Meditation practices, jhanas, conventional lifestyles, and various other techniques can provide temporary relief from mental distress without addressing the root causes of suffering. As a result, the need to seek happiness and peace arises again for those who do not possess such qualities such as ordinary people in monasteries and homes.

Experience of a Sotapanna's mind state substantially differ from an ordinary mind state. Once you have experienced the best, you do not seek anything more, and that is human nature. Having previously experienced limitless happiness as a Sotapanna, and having felt incomparable joy and peace as an Anagami, an Arahant becomes free from desires after having experienced the best of the world. This is how universal Nirvana is designed to meet human needs and nature, in accordance with Dhamma Niyama.

Thoughts continue to arise repeatedly until one experience the fourfold Nirvana and the cycle of samsara through this process. As Nibbana pertains to human nature, human beings are born with a tendency to grasp and seek pleasures, such as sensory pleasures. Even when a person follows rules or precepts, they still have an underlying tendency for sensory pleasures.

On the noble path, which is based on human nature, one does not have to compulsorily avoid sexual relations. Instead, individuals can maintain these relationships within the framework of the middle way, depending on personal choice. An Anagami gives up sensual pleasures, but this does not apply to a Sotapanna by nature. As people naturally let go of certain cravings over time, the middle path offers a comfortable and practical approach.

Moreover, when developing the noble path, a person does not need to close their eyes to avoid seeing things; rather, they need to understand that what they see is subject to change. A person must understand beyond interpreting their self and life experience based on conventions. Similarly, when a person understands Arahantship, they escape from grasping onto self, sensual pleasures, and other fetters. In this way, Nirvana Dhamma becomes a natural realization.

"And how does a noble disciple guard the sense doors? When a noble disciple sees a sight with their eyes, they don't get caught up in the features and details due to abandoning the desires; likes and dislikes for worldly experiences. If the faculty of sight were left unrestrained due to desires, bad unskillful qualities of covetousness and displeasure would become overwhelming. For this reason, they possess noble virtues based on right view, they naturally have the ability to protecting the faculty of sight (what they see don't impact them) and achieving its restraint due to no desires. When they hear a sound with their ears ... When they smell an odor with their nose ...

...And how does a noble disciple have seven good qualities? It's when a noble disciple has confirmed confidence in the Realized One's awakening: 'That Blessed One is perfected, a fully awakened Buddha, accomplished in knowledge and conduct, holy, knower of the world, supreme guide for those who wish to train, teacher of gods and humans, awakened, blessed."

- Sekhasutta, MN 53

Chapter 35:
Right living

To establish noble wisdom for many, it is crucial to explore how ordinary members within monastic communities behave and conduct themselves in their daily lives.

Right living is part of the Noble Eightfold Path. Sometimes, people tend to admire and respect those who live an ascetic lifestyle. However, this admiration can lead individuals who harbor greed, hatred, and delusion in monastic settings to misinterpret and misrepresent the teachings of Dhamma, including the universal Nirvana Dhamma. When honor, donations, money, or titles are given to those with such negative qualities, they are likely to misuse these resources. This can result in a deterioration of the purity of the Sangha within the community.

Often, discussions focus on what right living means for the ordinary sangha living in homes, but rarely is there conversation about what right living entails for the ordinary Sangha in monasteries. Right living for the ordinary Sangha involves developing the right view, sharing that view with others or their followers, and engaging in the practices of dana, sila, and bhavana. There are various kinds of dana. Among those who live in monasteries, dana refers to the act of sharing the right view with others without expecting anything in return, similar to what Arahants do, and sharing resources with others. To achieve this, one must progress through the four stages of the noble Nirvana Dhamma. Sila refers to the development of noble virtues that align with a Sotapanna (stream-enterer) and becoming free from the need to rely solely on monastic rules to maintain noble behavior. Bhavana involves cultivating an understanding of the universal Triple Gem, enabling individuals to share companionship with the universal Triple Gem. This raises the question: why would a person need companionship? The need for safety, security, and protection is a basic human need and this need is fulfilled through right companionship.

Non-noble companionship provides conventional friendships, while noble companionship offers friendship, care, and protection that transcends beyond conventions, individual's life experiences and the cycle of samsara. Most spiritual friends in monasteries do not develop these necessary aspects, which can hinder their potential to experience of Nirvana Dhamma. However, if they cultivate the right view and build upon it, they can begin to engage in right living. This principle applies in any setting. For instance, giving food satisfies hunger, providing water quells thirst, and sharing conventional Dhamma offers temporary relief. However, sharing the universal Nirvana Dhamma enables one to experience liberation from daily suffering. For the purpose of experiencing universal Nirvana Dhamma, you may build an association with noble friends.

Those living in a monastic setting, developing the right view includes reducing attachment and grasping the fetters, explain Dhamma across four stages of Nirvana Dhamma accurately without making errors, yet, many among those who live in monasteries do not develop the right view, and they may consume large amounts of donations not for the community benefit but for themselves, indicating a need for improvement in this area.

Chapter 36:
Saint is a mind state

In the contemporary context, spiritual friends do not hear the Dhamma directly from the lord of universal Dhamma, the universal Buddha. As a result, they have developed various misunderstandings of the Dhamma.

A common misconception about a saint in Buddha's path is that a saint is someone who can be identified externally. In this case, if external circumstances change, the perception of sainthood can also change. Instead, a noble saint on the Buddha's path is someone who has relinquished the deluded understanding that money, family, friends, and material possessions are stable, along with the underlying tendency to cling to such things in the mind.

"Suppabuddha, the leper, while sitting at the back of the crowd and listening attentively to the discourse given by the Buddha, attained Sotapatti Fruition."

-Dhp 66

Anyone from any background should follow the same practice of aligning with the rhythm of the universe (karma), which involves a commitment to purity in mind state.

"And how does a noble disciple guard the sense doors? When a noble disciple sees a sight with their eyes, they don't get caught up in the features and details due to abandoning the desires; likes and dislikes for worldly experiences..."

- Sekhasutta, MN 53

If someone is afraid that when they hear sounds or see sights, their desires will arise, this fear-based mindset reflects an ordinary mental state. Instead, one may develop a right-view mindset to reduce excessive desires based on deluded understanding in both the presence and absence of material things and worldly experiences.

"And what is right view? Right view, I tell you, is of two sorts: There is right view with effluents, siding with merit, resulting in acquisitions [of becoming]; there is right view that is noble, without effluents, transcendent, a factor of the path."

- Maha-cattarisaka Sutta, MN 117

Chapter 37: Grasping

For an ordinary person, developing the right view involves deepening the understanding that both the self and societal conventions are subject to change, and that Nirvana Dhamma is a universal occurrence based on one's karma and merits. This can be explained as follows.

Among spiritual friends, those seeking to experience blissful Nirvana Dhamma may learn to let go of their grasping self-view and conventions to begin with based on understanding both self and conventions are subject to change. They can develop right view to let go of deluded understanding of self and the society by taking refuge in or prioritizing the universal Triple Gem.

You may prioritize the universal Buddha more than any Sangha you know, or even family and friends. This is how you truly take refuge in the Buddha. Prioritize the Dhamma over following the opinions and actions of others. Recognize that social practices are not perfect and take responsibility for engaging in Dhamma-based thinking and actions in your daily activities. This is how you renounce social practices in Buddha's path. Practicing the Dhamma cannot hurt you or another. If something mentally hurts you or another, try and reflect that it is because you have not applied the true Dhamma. As much as possible, try to establish mindfulness based on the correct understanding of universal Dhamma to reduce deluded understanding of worldly experiences related to self in your daily life. When you give priority to your thoughts grasping the self-view (or the fetters) over the Dhamma, you will inevitably suffer. Instead, if you give priority to the Dhamma meaning renounce grasping the fetters more than yourself meaning grasping to self-view, your pain will subside. By prioritizing Dhamma, try to learn to renounce strains coming from life's pressures. In addition, remember that when you give priority to the conventional Sangha—such as monks, nuns, and spiritual friends who are ordinary in their mental state—your knowledge of the Dhamma and the merits you gain will remain low. However, when you prioritize the universal Sangha, meaning those who have transformed into becoming a direct disciple of the Buddha through past paramis and have let go of attachments to ten fetters, your understanding of the higher Dhamma will grow, and your merits will enhance.

"Companions, a companion should be a seeker of universal

Dhamma, an inquirer of universal Sangha, unable to comprehend another's mind, should scrutinize the Realized One for two things—things that can be seen and heard: 'Can anything corrupt (i.e grasping to conventional lifestyle) be seen or heard in the Realized One or
not?' Scrutinizing him they find that nothing corrupt can be seen or heard in the Realized One.

They scrutinize further: 'Can anything mixed (i.e., clinging to conventions; ritual, tradition, etc.) be seen or heard in the Realized One or not?' Scrutinizing him they find that nothing mixed can be seen or heard in the Realized One.

They scrutinize further: 'Can anything clean be seen or heard (i.e., likes, dislikes, expectations for worldly experiences; clinging to the past, sharing personal stories etc.) in the Realized One or not?' Scrutinizing him they find that clean things can be seen and heard in the Realized One.

They scrutinize further: 'Did the venerable attain this skillful state a long time ago, or just recently?' Scrutinizing him they find that the venerable attained this skillful state a long time ago, not just recently.
They scrutinize further: 'Are certain dangers (i.e., grasping conventions and are they mentally attached to fame, honor, possessions, friends, supporters, etc.) found in that person

who claims to gain Arahantship who has achieved fame and renown?' For, companions, so long as a person has not achieved fame and renown, certain dangers are not found in them. But when they achieve fame and renown, those dangers appear.

Scrutinizing him they find that those dangers are not found in that venerable individual who has achieved fame and renown.

They scrutinize further: 'Is this venerable securely stilled or insecurely stilled (i.e., do they refrain from sensuality as a practice, a part of sila or due to abandoning the relevant fetter)? Is the reason they don't indulge in sensual pleasures that they're free of greed because greed has ended?' Scrutinizing him they find that that venerable is securely stilled, not insecurely stilled stilled (i.e., do they refrain from sensuality due to fear of samsara or due to fearlessness of samsara and abandoning the relevant fetter)? The reason they don't indulge in sensual pleasures is that they're free of greed because greed has ended.

-MN 47, Vīmaṁsakasutta

"Friends, I don't say that Arahantship is achieved right away. Rather, Arahantship is achieved by gradual training, progress, and practice. And how is Arahantship is achieved by gradual training, progress, and practice?

It's when someone in whom faith has arisen approaches the Buddha or an Arahant (or at least a Sotapanna). They pay homage, actively listen, hear the four stages of Nibbana and the practice, remember things related to four stages of Nibbana and the practice, reflect on the practice and Nibbana, and accept them after deliberation. Then enthusiasm springs up; they make an effort, weigh up, and persevere. Persevering, they directly realize the ultimate truth, and see it with penetrating wisdom.

Friends, there has not been that faith, that approaching, that paying homage to the Buddha or an Arahant (or at least a Sotapanna) in their thoughts, that listening, that hearing the teachings, that remembering things related to four stages of Nibbana and the practice, that reflecting on their meaning, that acceptance after deliberation, that enthusiasm, that making an effort, that weighing up, or that striving. You're on a bad path, friends! You're practicing the wrong way! How far these futile men have strayed from this teaching and training!

There is an exposition in four statements, which a sensible person would quickly understand when it is recited. I shall recite it for you. Try to understand it."

"Sir, who are we next to those who understand the teaching?"

"Even with an ordinary monk, or a teacher who values external things, and things of the flesh such as lifestyles, traditions and conventions, is an heir in things of the flesh, who lives caught up in things of the flesh, you wouldn't get into such haggling: 'If we get this, we'll do that. If we don't get this, we won't do it.' What then of the Realized One, Arahants who lives utterly detached from things of the flesh?

For a faithful ordinary disciple who is practicing to fathom the Buddha or Arahant's instructions, this is in line with the teaching: 'The Buddha is my Teacher, I am his disciple. The Buddha and Arahants know, I do not know.' For a faithful ordinary disciple who is practicing to fathom Buddha and Arahant's instructions, Buddha and Arahant's instructions are nourishing and nutritious.

For a faithful disciple who is practicing to fathom the Buddha and Arahant's instructions, this is in line with the teaching: 'Gladly, let only skin, sinews, and bones remain!

Let the flesh and blood waste away in my body! I will not relax my energy until I have achieved what is possible by human strength, energy, and vigor.'

For a faithful disciple who is practicing to fathom the Buddha and Arahant's instructions, one of two results can be expected: Arahantship in this very life, or if there's something left over, non-return."

- Kīṭāgirisutta, MN 70

The common misunderstanding of a saint is that they must be someone who avoids money, does not associate with family and friends, and wears a specific robe as seen from the outside. However, a noble saint in Buddha's path is someone who has given up the delusion or deluded understanding that money, family, friends, and robes are not stable, along with the underlying tendency to cling to such things in their mind. In other words, understanding life experiences with wisdom is the practice of Dhamma, not merely focusing on external factors. This explains why the noble path begins with Right View. On the other hand, someone who maintains precepts out of fear of the potential to do unwholesome actions is considered an ordinary individual. If one fears that hearing sounds or seeing sights will trigger one's desires, this fear-based mindset reflects an ordinary mental state.

Instead, you can develop a mindset based on right view to help reduce desires, whether or not material things and worldly experiences are present. A person who has let go of these attachments does not need rules or precepts because they have gained the right view. This is how you should understand higher Dhamma.

Chapter 38:
The stand-alone practice among Arahants

Entering modern-day monastic settings can lead to the fading of universal Nirvana Dhamma. This happens because most monasteries explain universal Dhamma incorrectly and adhere to rules and hierarchies that are not conducive to preserving the universal Dhamma. Therefore, Arahants stand independently, regardless of their environment, simply to represent universal Nirvana Dhamma, which transcends conventional social practices. When one encounters Dhamma that goes beyond standard social norms, a sensible person should understand that it represents universally applicable Buddha's Dhamma, not merely a superficial imitation.

In Buddha's path, experiencing higher stages of Nibbana transforms a person into a monk within their mental continuum. With regard to the practice, an ordinary person may consciously strive to turn their intentions into wholesome actions in their mind.

Chapter 39:
The declaration of Arahantship

The Universal Buddha declared his attainment of enlightenment for the well-being of others. In the same way, Arahants either self-declare or should be recognized by the Buddha, allowing others the opportunity to accumulate merits and develop wisdom through their presence. This declaration is not meant to deceive or to gain material rewards for oneself. In truth, when a true Arahant receives anything, they share it with others, as they have relinquished desires for such possessions. This practice, recommended by the Buddha, encourages mutual support on the path to extinguishment.

Anyone who attains cessation should self-declare their Arahantship and share their insights, so that others may have the opportunity to experience the same. The Great Arahant Mahinda, Arahant Sanghamitta, and many other Arahants, including some from today, have self-declared their Arahantship in accordance with the teachings of the Supreme Buddha, solely to benefit the Sangha.

The Declaration of Arahantship serves a greater purpose within the Buddha's path. It provides fellow practitioners an opportunity to contemplate the noble wisdom and qualities of the enlightened ones, which can help generate wholesome thoughts, enhance merits, and cultivate wisdom. This is why the Buddha encourages ordinary Sangha to reflect on the noble wisdom and qualities of the noble Sangha.

Chapter 40:
Attachment

Lack of understanding of Nibbana, the practice, and the Dhamma can hinder the realization of Nibbana. If Nibbana were solely linked to a monastic lifestyle, then most, if not all, those who live a monastic lifestyle would experience the four-fold Nibbana. However, this is not the case, indicating that solely adhering to a monastic lifestyle is not a reliable way to attain Nibbana. The same applies to those living a non-monastic lifestyle. Nibbana is not defined by external factors or lifestyle choices. One can live a certain lifestyle while still holding onto deluded understandings within the mind. Instead, Nibbana is a transformation of the mind state.

Dhamma matters are related to mind states or the mental continuum of a being. By focusing more attention to understanding mind states, one can put more effort into making progress in Buddha's path, which caters to a person's mental continuum. In the Buddha's path, renunciation means letting go of the ten fetters. By releasing these fetters, one diminishes desires for oneself, others, and the world, which are often rooted in deluded understanding. Therefore, desires can be lessened through the correct understanding of the mind, regardless of external factors.

You cannot understand Nibbana just because you live in a monastic setting. You have to understand how your thoughts in your mind work. The mind by default can get attached to things. For example, if you were to live in a monastic setting (or non-monastic setting), you can get attached to things such as the meditation hall, peace in a forest, the monastery (or the house, the friends) and the like. If you slowly train the mind to understand when your mind gets attached to such things and, each time as it happens over time, by reflecting the consequences of such attachment meaning reflecting how, when you get hold into your thoughts of the world (monastery, family, self, friends, world, economy, politics, etc.), these things can make you feel worried, anxious, depressed, sad, and upset about the very same things. They are not worth the pain, as they change anyway. That is how you can awaken the mind to see the truth and train to blissful Sotapanna.

An Arahant sees their real-time thoughts naturally as if one sees thoughts on a separate sheet or on the screen of an iPad with the understanding that they are not stable or permanent. Not having the desire for one's thoughts makes one free from pain. To come to such a state, one must develop stream entry first. In preparation for that, one may take steps to shape one's thoughts in line with Dhamma in daily life.

If you can train your mind to understand things beyond common ways of understanding with wisdom, and see your thoughts as they run across everywhere, as if they are in a separate sheet or an iPad or an x-ray, it will help you reduce attachment to your thoughts and renounce the world. In this way, as you recollect Dhamma when you experience distress in daily life, you can slowly let go of deluded understanding over time.

Chapter 41: Self-view

Developing the noble path across the four stages of Nirvana Dhamma requires understanding "self-view" and other fetters, as well as gaining a deeper understanding of the universal Buddha, universal Dhamma, and universal Sangha in accordance with the insights of the noble Ones. Ordinary Sangha, or spiritual friends in monasteries and homes can learn and understand more about the universal Triple Gem beyond what they already know.

Apart from observing your thoughts and learning to let go of grasping self-view and conventions to begin with, it is essential to develop a correct understanding of the perfect Buddha, perfect Dhamma, and perfect Sangha to experience stream entry (Sotapanna).

Understanding the perfect qualities of the universal Triple Gem will help you release your attachments, which is what we mean by taking refuge in the universal Triple Gem on the noble path. This does not simply mean uttering the phrases "I take refuge in the Triple Gem" or “I take refuge in the Buddha, Dhamma, and Sangha" without a true understanding of what the Triple Gem represents. Those who seek Nirvana Dhamma and consider themselves followers of the Buddha or outside disciples should strive to understand the universal Buddha, universal Dhamma, and the universal Sangha is beneficial for experiencing the state of Sotapanna. The more you come to understand the Triple Gem, the more you can develop a profound understanding of universal Nirvana Dhamma and cultivate the right view on the Noble Path. This deepening of understanding will bring you closer to achieving universal Nirvana and practicing Dhamma.

Developing the right understanding of the noble path involves grasping the significance of the Dhamma and the Sangha in accordance with the insights of the noble ones, which you can learn by listening to the Dhamma from noble friends or Arahants. Spiritual friends and ordinary Sangha in monasteries and homes can learn and understand more about the universal Triple Gem beyond what they already know.

Social ordination is temporary, and one must leave it behind at the time of death. Universal ordination transcends birth and death. Ordination refers to the process of letting go of ten fetters across four stages of universal

Nirvana Dhamma. You can learn to comprehend the way to release self-view, social practices, and understand the universal Triple Gem to experience Sotapanna. In previous discussions, I've explained how to train in letting go of grasping at self-view and social practices. Here, I will discuss how you can understand the universal Triple Gem, which is an essential aspect of training that you need to develop right view on the noble path.

First, to understand the universal Buddha, recognize that he embodies the best of wisdom and perfect qualities, serving as the teacher of all perfected beings. It is also important to be aware that some individuals have deliberately misinterpreted the higher Dhamma, which misrepresents the perfect Buddha and makes him appear imperfect. It's essential to identify when these misrepresentations of the Buddha come to your attention. For instance, some ordinary Sangha members in monastic settings praise men while downgrading women, claiming that women must respect men simply for being men. This creates a distorted image of the Buddha and is a wrong interpretation. There should be no doubts: there is no one in this world who wishes to treat, respect and protect the well-being of women as much as the Supreme Buddha does. This understanding reflects the perfect wisdom and infinite kindness of the universal Buddha. Not only women but also men, as well as all beings, deserve to be treated with respect, care and protection. This is a fundamental lesson that the Supreme Buddha taught us, his universal disciples. You can also learn to cultivate these noble qualities within yourself. This can be discussed as below:

Rules are not essential if the Sangha can develop a noble view. You may keep certain rules if they help you reduce unwholesome behaviors, but strive to go beyond monastic rules or precepts by cultivating the right view of a Sotapanna. When one possesses the noble view, noble virtues will naturally follow. This explains why, during the time of the Supreme Buddha, he did not establish any fixed rules. The rules included in the Pali Canon were introduced gradually and only to prevent excessive and inappropriate behavior among ordinary people or members of the Sangha living in monasteries. There are gaps that need to be filled in order to interpret existing sources in line with the four stages of Nirvana Dhamma. It is important to understand that grasping at form represents a departure from Dhamma practice. In contrast, reducing attachment to form aligns with practicing Dhamma.

The Buddha's Dhamma and Vinaya refer to the four sages of Nirvana Dhamma and the four types of disciples: Sotapanna, Sakadagami, Anagami, and Arahant. Buddha's footprint, found in his noble disciples, transcends limited conventions. This is how you should understand the teacher of perfected ones, both humans and gods, universal Buddha.

In addition, if someone claims that men are better, the same as, or worse than women or vice versa, they are only suggesting part of their nature is superior, similar, or inferior to the other part. This is because all men and woman are created by a mother and a father, and in that sense, both men and women are integral to everyone's nature. While certain characteristics of a particular form may be better suited for specific roles, this suitability does not mean that one's form is superior, same or inferior to another. This is because the form of even the strongest men and women do not remain the same; they are subject to change. Grasping form is practicing non-dhamma. Not grasping, or at least reducing grasping, is practicing Dhamma.

Universal Buddhas and his disciple Arahants don't grasp at anything, this explains why words are mere words for an Arahant. For example, by being a good parent, one man and woman may be able to gift a child to society through parenthood, while another man may offer basics of the teachings of the Buddha as an ordinary monk, another man may offer cleaning services as a cleaner, and another woman may provide legal services as a lawyer or share their musical talents. Whenever anyone contributes in their own way to the well-being of themselves and others, they are practicing the Dhamma trough their efforts in contributing to the society. This explains why there are no unusual things to do in the noble path but to apply wisdom, and noble qualities within your daily roles, and daily activities. Conventional Sangha may explain the basic Dhamma and introduce you to preliminary Dhamma practices. In contrast, the noble Sangha will explain the higher Dhamma, including the four stages of universal Nirvana. However, this is not meant to suggest that one is superior, inferior, or the same as the other; rather, in the path leading to extinguishment, cessation or Nirvana, it is about merely using Dhamma and Sangha for their intended purpose without grasping or hurting anyone. This is how you should understand perfect qualities of the universal Nirvana Dhamma as taught by the buddha.

Using resources for unwholesome acts does not align with the Dhamma, regardless of whether one touches money in public or not. For example, if one uses science to make weapons and harm people, that is non-Dhamma. Conversely, if one uses science to enhance happiness, health, and well-being for people, that is Dhamma. If someone becomes a parent and is a toxic parent, that is non-Dhamma. However, if a person is a good parent, that is practicing Dhamma. If someone, as an ordinary monk, shares a wrong view, that is non-Dhamma. If someone becomes a Sotapanna and shares the right view, that is higher Dhamma in practice. When an Arahant shares higher Dhamma, that is Dhamma in action. Whenever one contributes to enhancing their own well-being and that of others, they are practicing Dhamma. When one provides others to develop the right view, with an opportunity to experience the fourfold Nirvana Dhamma, that is higher Dhamma in action. In the noble path, action alone is not sufficient; intentional action is crucial. In line with universal law of Dhamma, the intentional actions of a person grasping the ten fetters shape their karma. Those who are free from the ten fetters do not produce new karma regardless of their actions. This is how you should understand higher Dhamma.

The next thing you should understand is that interpreting the Sangha through conventional perspectives does not align with the Noble Path. When you understand Dhamma and Sangha based on conventions, you adopt an ordinary view rather than the "right view" of the noble path. Instead, one should learn to understand Dhamma and Sangha matters beyond mere conventions.

To understand the noble path, recognize that there are two categories of disciples: outsiders and insiders. Outsider disciples include ordinary monks, ordinary nuns, and male and female householders. They are bound to samsara as they cling to ten fetters. Insiders, on the other hand, have transcended conventional limitations and include the Sotapanna, Sakadagami, Anagami, and Arahant.

Chapter 42:
Beyond conventions

In the context of the noble path, the term "lay" refers to Sotapanna and Sakadagamis. In this path, the term "monk" specifically refers to Arahants. In ordinary terms, "monk" can refer to anyone who receives social ordination. In the noble path, "monk" denotes someone who has completed universal ordination shaped by karma and merits that ultimately ends birth, death, and the cycle of samsara regardless of external factors. This is how you should understand and interpret the matters of Dhamma and Sangha in line with the noble path.

Chapter 43:
Not structures, but the final body

One myth is the belief that the Buddha's universal disciples, who have completed the four stages of Nirvana Dhamma, can only exist in a monastic setting or an environment constructed of cement and other materials. it is important to understand that monasticism on the noble path is not merely about an external environment; it relates to the final body bearded by an Arahant. This clarifies why the Buddha recommended that when people of noble linage or Buddhahood gained through various ways such as Tathagata, Paccekabuddha, and Arahant dies, monuments should be erected for them so that such monuments provide both trainees (i.e. Sotapanna, Sakadagami, Anagami) and outsider disciples (ordinary monks, nuns, ordinary householders) the opportunity to gather merit by honoring these figures, thereby creating a place of worship. The terms "insider" and "outsider" are used merely to explain higher Dhamma, not to claim that one is superior, equal, or inferior to another on the path leading to extinction or cessation. Understanding this is essential for developing the right view on the noble path, which aligns with what the noble ones comprehend.

Chapter 44: Infant Dhamma

Over the centuries, spiritual practitioners have often described Dhamma at an elementary level. Dhamma at this infancy level refers to explaining Dhamma as concepts, quotes, and similar ways without any reference to the four stages of Nirvana. For example, spiritual practitioners often suggest engaging in meditations without accurately explaining which type of meditation is required for each state of Nirvana Dhamma. They may refer to knowledge that has been understood for centuries without acknowledging what lies beyond common knowledge. Commonly known practices within Dhamma include chanting parittas, reading discourses, participating in rituals, and understanding Dhamma merely as concepts or meditation practices, including jhana practices, dress codes, and the influence of external factors. Anyone who explains universal Dhamma in simple terms is discussing it at an elementary level. But why would an Arahant explain Dhamma at this level? The reason is that there are very few spiritual practitioners who are at an elementary level, both in monasteries and at home. By teaching at this level,

Arahants assure these learners that they are already conversant in basic Dhamma and aim to help those who are still learning to progress further from where they are.

This brings us to the question: what is higher Dhamma? Higher Dhamma refers to teaching how to attain the four stages of Nirvana and explaining how a person can develop the mind to go beyond common ways or achieve the status of a Sotapanna.

One important thing to remember is that to practice as a Sotapanna, one needs to integrate Dhamma into daily life. In other words, it is vital to apply wisdom and cultivate noble qualities in our everyday activities, as discussed in previous posts. If you treat Dhamma as separate from your typical daily routines, the strength of your Dhamma practice may not be sufficient to enable you to incorporate it into your normal activities. Thus, you can learn how to apply Dhamma within your usual social roles and daily activities, as discussed earlier.

Nirvana Dhamma has four stages, and it requires expanding and discussing these ideas. However, rarely does anyone provide this explanation, leading spiritual practitioners in monasteries and non-monasteries to stagnate on the noble path. By understanding the practices needed to develop the four stages of Nirvana, a spiritual practitioner can cultivate a right understanding of the practice and achieve the right view, which is the first stage of the noble path. A person aspiring for Nibbana must learn beyond these preliminary levels of Dhamma to precisely understand how to practice in a manner that leads to Nibbana. Nirvana Dhamma has four stages, and it is not experienced through jhanas as a single instance of enlightenment.

In addition, most practitioners tend to treat Dhamma as a separate practice from their daily lives; they might feel the need to retreat or go to monasteries to practice, which only captures the preliminary aspects. Instead, one must learn to apply Dhamma as an integral part of their normal life and daily activities. In this way, if someone can explain the limitations of existing common Dhamma practices, identify gaps, and teach you how to link and expand upon what you already know, they are offering more than what you already understand. Someone who is able to explain the four stages of Nirvana Dhamma in depth, along with the necessary practices and reasoning, represents the universal Buddha's Dhamma. Anyone who conveys this universal understanding is representing the universal Sangha. This is the essence of higher Dhamma and its significance.

Chapter 45: Misinterpreting Dhamma, it is not the action

There is a widely spread myth suggesting that someone who is socially ordained should not disclose their attainment of Nirvana to someone who is not socially ordained. This belief is an erroneous view and misinterpreting Dhamma. The reason can be explained as below:

Declaration is an act, but the act itself is not central to Buddha's Dhamma; rather, it is the intentionality behind the act that holds significance. This means that anyone who declares they have experienced Arahantship with the intention of gaining benefits for themselves—whether from a socially ordained person or from others—should refrain from such intentional actions. This clarifies why individuals like Arahant Angulimala, Arahant Mahinda, and Arahant Sangamitta could declare Arahantship.

The intention behind one's actions is crucial in the noble path. Instead, this rule should be interpreted as follows: anyone in a monastic setting who falsely declares their attainment of a Sotapanna, Sakadagi, Anagami, or

Arahant with the intent to gain benefits for themselves must avoid such declarations. Intentional actions based on unwholesome or falsified Dhamma and Sangha matters should be avoided.

The intent to gain benefits can only arise in the mind of an ordinary person, not in the mind of an Arahant. This is why the Vinaya Pitaka is primarily for the ordinary Sangha and is not applicable to Arahants, even in monastic settings. However, Arahants in monastic settings will still meet and recite the monastic rules for the purpose of training the ordinary Sangha, as it assists them in avoiding unwholesome actions, not because they need it for themselves. This is how you should understand it.

Everything in the noble path must be interpreted in line with the four stages of Nirvana Dhamma. If Dhamma is interpreted in a way that conflicts with these four stages, it goes against the teachings of the Buddha.

Typically, many ordinary members of the Sangha misunderstand the Buddha's teachings simply because they do not know how to walk the path of the Buddha. This understanding is often only gained by those who have actually walked the path. Even if someone attempts to describe Dhamma through imitation, they cannot accurately convey it in line with the four stages of Nirvana

Dhamma. This is why spiritual practitioners often do not experience Nirvana; it is not a matter of merely attaining a certain appearance or following a model. Instead, it involves developing inner wisdom and qualities.

Appearance of Arahants are rare. One must learn from spiritual friends who are Arahants to understand the teachings of the Buddha precisely. Otherwise, Sangha members who stray from universal teachings move away from the Noble Path. However, by gaining a deeper understanding of the fourfold Nibbana beyond what you already know, you can better comprehend the universal Buddha, Dhamma, and Sangha. It is through understanding the universal Triple Gem that you can experience the fourfold Nirvana Dhamma and vice versa.

Chapter 46:
The reason for Dhamma

By their nature, all beings have needs. There is a reason why a human being or person wants to follow Dhamma, and that is to fulfill a need. Human nature dictates that when one is hungry, one eats food; when one is thirsty, one drinks water. Similarly, when one feels miserable, sad, or lonely, one needs to reflect on and apply Dhamma to alleviate such feelings. However, when the Dhamma you've known for centuries does not provide remedies for your daily needs or resolve your pains, you tend to overlook its value.

Let's say you eat something, but it does not satisfy your hunger or taste. You wouldn't be too much interested in it anymore. In the same way, if the Dhamma you've encountered has not been able to resolve your mental stress completely or at least help you feel some sense of equanimity, you might often forget about Dhamma by nature and prioritize other aspects of life instead.

This explains why in general, in seeking happiness, most spiritual practitioners give priority to various things that are not Dhamma. Most members of the ordinary Sangha, whether in monasteries or at home, tend to seek happiness in activities that are not directly related to the four stages of Nirvana Dhamma. These activities include attending events such as conferences, visiting places, studying Dhamma as an academic subject, watching movies, participating in sports, and engaging in entertainment. While some individuals practice meditation as a separate activity, fewer people know how to apply Dhamma in their daily activities, which allows them to experience peace and happiness in life. Many practitioners are unaware of the benefits they can gain from universal Nirvana Dhamma. This brings us to a crucial question: How can one make Buddha's Dhamma effective enough to address the daily needs of human beings while allowing them to do usual activities? Experiencing the four stages of Nirvana Dhamma addresses a fundamental need. In this context, the next question is: How can one practice Dhamma to experience its benefits? First and foremost, an ordinary person must focus on reducing grasping self-view and conventions in daily life while reflecting on the qualities of the noble Triple Gem and maintaining noble virtues. This brings us to question; why is it important to include the aspect of the Universal Triple Gem?

From a need's perspective, beings naturally have a need for safety and protection, which is fulfilled through right companionship on the noble path. Non-noble companionship may offer conventional friendships, but your need for companionship may not be satisfied through such relationships. In contrast, noble companionship offers friendship, care, and protection that transcend conventional boundaries. You can experience this while alive, without needing to wait until you die to encounter the blissful state of Nirvana. If someone tells you that you have to wait until your death to experience certain things, that sounds like a fairy tale. The truth is not a fantasy; it's something you should be able to experience while you are alive and living your daily life. Spiritual friends in monasteries need to develop wisdom through the stages of Nirvana and cultivate noble qualities. This observation holds true in any setting. May all friends cultivate noble wisdom and noble qualities as they seek and strive for the four stages of universal Nirvana Dhamma in their spiritual journeys. I have clarified matters related to universal Nirvana Dhamma beyond what you already know. You may develop the right view, share it with your followers, and contribute towards fostering a noble sangha community.